ARCHITECTURE OF THE 20TH CENTURY IN DRAWINGS

UTOPIA AND REALITY

ARCHITECTURE OF THE 20TH CENTURY IN DRAWINGS

UTOPIA AND REALITY

Vittorio Magnago Lampugnani

RIZZOLI NEW YORK

Library of Congress Cataloging in Publication Data

Magnago Lampugnani, Vittorio, 1951 –
  The architecture of the 20th century in drawings.

  Translation of: Architektur unseres Jahrhunderts in
Zeichnungen.
  Bibliography: p.
  Includes index.
  1. Architectural drawing – 20th century. I. Title.
II. Title: Architecture of the twentieth century in drawings.
NA2700.M3513   1982   720'.22'2   82–42534
ISBN 0-8478-0464-X

Translation into English: Eileen Martin
Revised by: Vittorio Magnago Lampugnani and Claude Lubroth

First published in the United States of America in 1982 by
RIZZOLI INTERNATIONAL PUBLICATIONS, INC.
712 Fifth Avenue, New York, NY 10019

ISBN: 0-8478-0464-X
LC: 82-42534

CONTENTS

"The design preserves the dream of the house; a glance through the window frames it. The model, too, stands as seen from far away, covered with a protective layer; though transparent, it permits no access or entry."
Ernst Bloch, *Das Prinzip Hoffnung*, 1938–59.

Architecture in its historical evolution can be shown in various ways. In words, with a text which outlines the development. In photographs, showing buildings which "make" history. Finally through drawings by architects.

There are three reasons for the last choice.

The decision in favour of architectural drawings eliminates the distinction between what has been built and what has not. The realisation of the project, which generally depends directly on economic circumstances, is no longer the conditio sine qua non of architecture. Through drawings and sketches it is possible to present architectural ideas tout court, thus preserving what is culturally valuable and would otherwise be lost in architectural consumption. This is of no little relevance, since "desk drawer architecture" is often artistically and historically as important as what has been built. There is no lack of examples of this: they range from Etienne Louis Boullée's Cenotaph for Newton through Ludwig Mies van der Rohe's early designs for glass towers to Superstudio's Monumento Continuo. The most decisive expression of the idea comes in bold Utopian designs which are divorced from any pressure of realisation. Creativity appears in its purest form, visions, unfettered by compromise, unfold freely. Apparently released from reality, their disruptive and stirring impulses contribute the most to changing it.

Moreover, architectural drawings are often the clearest indication of the genesis of a project. The basic idea leaves its mark on the paper, while the further stages of the work are visible as superimposed layers. The creative process decodes itself like a geological formation.

Finally, architectural drawings can often express more than finished buildings. Technique, manner of presentation, cut, format, handling of line and trend are all revelatory of the artist's intellectual intent. Drawings of architecture are consequently testimonies to cultural attitudes; passionate as they are exact, they take on an independent artistic value and can stand in their own right as autonomous works.

Autonomous works in the general body of architecture: these are projects which have been designed and actually have been built; projects which were designed to be built but for some reason never were; and finally projects which were conceived in the knowledge that they would never be realised but were still intended as an intellectual contribution to architecture – Antonio Sant'Elia's visions of the Città Nuova, for example. Not included are architectural drawings whose main function is to make a contribution to graphics or painting. Certainly the borders are fluid, because an aesthetically valuable drawing for an architectural project is necessarily bound to extend into the "free arts". Nevertheless, the aim has been to draw the distinction where the architectural engagement is subordinated to the involvement in graphic art or painting.

In this context the problem of direct authorship is also less crucial. The authenticity of the signature plays a major part in a painting but not in an architectural drawing. Of course here too there is a concern with technique, the handling of line, the "master's touch". But whether the master really executed a drawing himself or whether, as is usual even in small offices, his staff did the work, is of only philological interest. Also in the "botteghe" of the Cinquecento it was usual for apprentices to carry out sections of works which were then signed by the master and fully accepted as his creation. In architectural drawing, where the instrumental component plays a greater role than the autonomous, this is even more legitimate. It does not touch the necessity of fair and exact information on the executants, of course; but an architect's intellectual product in the wider sense should be interpreted broadly.

This selection of drawings covers the period from 1910 to the present; the main emphasis is on contemporary works. The single drawings have been grouped into streams or directions and within these arranged chronologically. However, this is not sustained schematically; it is interrupted wherever it appeared that comparisons would be valuable or informative. The architectural streams themselves are also arranged chronologically, as far as the dialectic of history with its parallelisms and counter-streams permits, and especially as far as the historical continuity of the streams themselves permits. Where there are several projects by one architect, the chronological order within the stream is broken to allow a coherent image of the personality. But if, as frequently happens, the work of one architect moves through several different trends, these are separated to show each single work in its own context.

Altogether, in the present survey, synthesis has been preferred to analysis, the overall view to concentration in depth; a decision that was made deliberately but not without unease. The same can be said of the choice of architects, which is bound to appear meagre and unjust, especially since the main criteria were not only good ideas and good buildings but also and indeed primarily good drawings. Ultimately, any and every historiographic structure, however carefully built up, must appear questionable and open to alternatives; even one which is as general as that proposed here.

Out of the rather bold attempt to give a survey in pictures of the architecture of seventy particularly feverish years in a book of normal size follows the imposition of a policy of severe selection. An attempt has been made to turn a necessity into a virtue and filter from the seemingly endless variety and range available those drawings which testify to a really creative struggle with the conditions of the time.

To give at least a rough insight into the cultural depth of this struggle and make some, albeit modest, contribution to its further development, the drawings are preceded by fragments of a critical history of architectural drawing in the 20th century. Thus the works are placed in their historical context and briefly commented.

Vittorio Magnago Lampugnani   Berlin, April 1982

My thanks go to Gerd Hatje and Axel Menges for the many patient and helpful discussions in the course of which, after more than two years' work, this book has reached its present form. I would also like to thank Matthias Groene and Karin Janthur for valuable help in acquiring the material. Finally I am also grateful to the many friends and acquaintances who willingly made their collections available.

V.M.L.

The art of architectural drawing retained the high standing it had enjoyed throughout the nineteenth century also in the period of Art Nouveau, in spite of all its revolutionary pressure to innovate, as the new style, with its vegetable forms and fluid lines, evocative of flames, waves, trails of flowers and wildly blowing hair, came to oppose academic historicism just before the turn of the century. In a sublimation of subjective emotion, which had its philosophical parallel in the works of Friedrich Nietzsche and Henri Bergson, architects like Victor Horta, Henry van de Velde, Hector Guimard, August Endell, Raimondo D'Aronco, Louis Comfort Tiffany, Charles Rennie Mackintosh, Otto Wagner, Joseph Maria Olbrich, Josef Hoffmann and Antoni Gaudí experimented with boldly and elegantly alienated natural forms used primarily for their aesthetic and expressive potential. Born as a revolutionary movement with progressive social claims, Art Nouveau, however, soon became the exclusive creative canon of the privileged progressives, presenting a refined mirror to the melancholy charm of the bourgeoisie.

The Myth of Nature as Model:
From Frank Lloyd Wright to Eero Saarinen

It was not coincidence that Frank Lloyd Wright began by taking up Art Nouveau, when in the 1890s he ushered in that far reaching reform which, under the name "organic", was to create in American architecture a true alternative to the classical European tradition. Certainly there were other influences which were purely American: the romantic world and ideas of Ralph Waldo Emerson, the extreme individualism of Henry David Thoreau, the naturism of Walt Whitman and the organic ideal of Horatio Greenough, writer and sculptor, who believed that he could localise the first "step down" in the fine arts in the "introduction of the first inorganic non-functional element."[1]

With this and the love of nature he developed at an early age on his grandfather's farm in Spring Green, Wisconsin, Wright set about conquering "America the Beautiful" with his architecture. Almost all his designs for houses are set in the country or its surrogate, the urban suburb. His gradual and symbolic occupation of the nation, though, which took him from Oak Park, near Chicago, to California, was directed with sensitivity and care. His buildings seem like parts of the landscape, from which they appear to grow in harmony, forms, colours and materials carefully attuned to their environment.

The heritage of nearly 8,000 architectural drawings left by Wright, who was obsessed with his work, are an impressive testimony to the range and intensity of his preoccupation.[2]

One is struck immediately by the naturalism and the immense care over detail. These are largely studies in perspective, and the buildings appear as they would to an observer, with no intellectual abstraction. The view is from the ground or the air, in order to show the organisation of the building better. The fine line drawings are coloured in pale, harmonising tones. In most cases the material to be used in the building is recognisable. For Wright the general impression of a building never depends primarily on the distribution of volume or geometrical laws or proportions, it is always a product of the architectural whole. Every detail (as in a "Gesamtkunstwerk", a total work of art) has the same significance as the overall form.

But for all their accessibility and apparent simplicity these drawings are not in any way vignettes for the sales market; they are a virtuoso execution of a revolutionary architectural concept. On every level it is clear that these are not only crystalline representations of an invented reality, they are at the same time a critical instrument with which to test and perfect this invention.

Particularly striking in Wright's drawings is the relation between nature and architecture. Both quantitatively and qualitatively the landscape plays a major role. In most of the drawings it frames the house completely, often taking up more of the surface space than the architecture itself and here and there actually bursting across the thinly sketched edge to stretch its exuberant growth on to the mount. Nature is an equal partner, if not indeed the main protagonist of the artistic creed. Drawn with the utmost care and precision, it is never a mere background or addition, always an essential complementary element to the house: without nature the house could not exist for it would lose both its model and its raison d'être.

It is hardly surprising that Wright's ideas and architectural visions were taken up in a country in which, as in the USA, nature is huge, wild and untamed, playing a primary role in the life of man: Finland. In 1949 Alvar Aalto, already world famous, wrote: "After all, nature is a symbol of freedom."[3]

As early as 1935 he had said: "Contact with nature and the variety nature always provides is a life form which gets on very uneasily with over-formalistic ideas... The objects that surround man are hardly mere fetishes and allegories with some mystical eternal value. They are more likely to be cells and tissues, alive just as cells and tissues are, the building components of which human life is composed. They cannot be dealt with in a different way from biology's other units, otherwise they would be in danger of becoming unsuited to the system, of becoming inhuman."[4]

Strongly influenced by his grandfather, Hugo Hamilkar Hackstedt, a grand bourgeois survivor of the eighteenth century intelligentsia, Aalto too remained all his life balanced between the scepticism of Voltaire, Rousseau's "natural" social concept and the exuberance of German idealism. He filled his life and work with myths, heroism, and Homeric drama. With the same proud self-confidence with which Wright spoke in the Arizona desert before the crackling altar flames to his assembled disciples, Aalto declared himself the patriarch of the modern movement in Finland – and he became it.

His architecture, like the architecture of Wright, is an abstract mimesis of nature, the buildings grow up from the ground, absorb the formal influences of the landscape and become part of their surroundings. Like Wright's houses they represent the anarchic myth of a virtually limitless personal freedom. And like Wright's creations they heighten their own constructive and functional conditions, they do not shy away from the great gesture but freely acknowledge their will towards nobility and grandeur.

Only on a superficial view may these common features not seem apparent in the drawings of Wright and Aalto.

What may seem bare and withered in Aalto's work, in utter contrast to Wright's intensely detailed renderings, on a closer examination reveals a strength which can certainly stand comparison with the work of the American pioneer. Building and landscape are only sketched in rough outline, but it is an abstraction which touches the essence. The lines are both searching and sure, cautious and strong, careful and bold. Colour is rare and it is not naturalistic, always symbolic. Even sheets worked out in most detail are only sketches, never perfected drawings. For Aalto, in fact, drawing was always a means to move through experiments and detours to the architectural form: an adventurous journey of intuition through space and time, an examination of the endless variety of form in the sphere of the organic.[5]

That so high a degree of individualism could at best produce followers but not a "school" in the real sense is inherent in its premises. However, some architects did follow the path taken by Wright and Aalto while remaining autonomous thinkers and creators.

One of the most important was Hugo Häring. With his theory of "organic building" and his attempts to mobilise expression and function "as equal partners"[6] he formed a kind of link between Expressionism and Rationalism. The result was to be "organic formations,"[7] not directly reflecting natural models but endeavouring to discover "the form which lies concealed in the thing itself."[8] But in his soft, generally perspectivist drawings Häring developed concepts which ultimately, despite his assurances to the contrary, do homage to a new formalism in their oblique angles, curved lines and arches shaped like flat-irons.

However, the tradition of organic architecture lived on even without a school: in the heretical splintered forms of Hans Scharoun, the exquisite craftsmanship of Carlo Scarpa, the bold swinging movement of Eero Saarinen. Even architects who appeared to be far removed from its world occasionally drew on this intellectual and formal repertoire: one was Le Corbusier, who sketched the chapel of Nôtre-Dame-du-Haut in Ronchamp with fine free strokes, an architectural gesture which is as arbitrary as it is fascinating and would have found even Greenough's approval.

The Breakthrough of Subjective Expression:
From Bruno Taut to Paolo Soleri

Not too remote from the forms of organic architecture were the restless and heterogeneous creations of architectural Expressionism, in which the element of the subjective forced its way into the foreground. Most of its protagonists shared with Frank Lloyd Wright and Carlo Scarpa a more or less obscure origin in the intellectual and aesthetical repertoire of Art Nouveau; but the roots of the real Expressionist movement are in the paintings of the Neue Künstlervereinigung founded in Munich 1909, one year after publication of Wilhelm Worringer's influential theoretical work *Abstraktion und Einfühlung*.

Expressionist architecture, which emerged largely independently in a number of places during the First World War and was represented by such different characters as Hans Poelzig and Rudolf Steiner, found a crystallisation point in the Arbeitsrat für Kunst, formed in 1918 under the leadership of Bruno Taut and Adolf Behne. The Arbeitsrat arranged lectures, published manifestos, leaflets and two small books, but its main purpose was to organise exhibitions: in 1919 the "Ausstellung für unbekannte Architekten" brought Hermann Finsterlin into contact with the Berlin association, while "Neues Bauen" in 1920 largely consisted of Taut's drawings for *Alpine Architektur* and *Der Weltbaumeister*.

In his 1919 book *Alpine Architektur* Taut, infected by the exuberant enthusiasm of his friend the poet Paul Scheerbart for glass as a building material, suggested an "Alpenbau" to transform the entire chain of mountains from the North Italian lakes to Monte Rosa into a fairy-tale landscape of glass sanctuaries and crystal druses. In "Erdrindenbau" he then proposed extending the action to every continent and in "Stern-

bau" into the cosmos. Behind the "glittering domes" and "sparkling palaces" lies the shadow of Nietzsche's megalomania. A year later came *Die Auflösung der Städte oder Die Erde eine gute Wohnung oder auch Der Weg zur Alpinen Architektur*, a fantastic illustration of the ideas of the anarchist Kropotkin on politics and urban design. Shortly afterwards the series of 28 charcoal drawings *Der Weltbaumeister* was published.

So Taut's drawings played a central part in the transmission of his early ideas. They are a striking mixture of clumsiness in detail and expertise in creating a particular mood and a general impression. Taut orients all the technique to the didactically effective presentation of these naively megalomanic projects which he conceived as parables. The drawings are simplified perspectives, "vedutas", drawn with enough abstraction to show the essential but sufficiently concrete to have the appeal of the vignette. There are several pictures, even to different scales, on one sheet; this is to show relations and stimulate comparison. There are time sequences in the arrangement, filmic changes from detail to the whole. And with it all there are intensive, carefully visualised inscriptions, with poignant use of colour and capital letters, the strokes varying in strength, the lines rhythmically arranged, allowing both a real geographical localisation for the fictive architectural interventions and an explanation of the meaning and purpose of the intervention itself. The insistence that "art should no longer be the pleasure of the few but the happiness and life of the mass"[9] makes the drawings intelligible to the layman. They are logically close to the bubble cartoons which had become popular in the United States since the end of the nineteenth century.

But Taut's "noble cartoons" never sacrifice artistic quality to pragmatism. The lively sheets with their searching lines, delicate colours and commentaries in an elaborate hand-writing full of emphatic exclamation marks radiate a refreshing and magically touching poetry in their unpretentious preciosity: this is the aestheticism of Art Nouveau filled with a new moralising power and thus undergoing a deep-rooted change.

The circle around Taut, which had already formed by the end of 1919 in the Utopian correspondence of the "Gläserne Kette", included many painter-architects who not only during the depression following the war, but throughout their lives never built at all. Among them were Paul Gösch, Wenzel August Hablik and Hermann Finsterlin, the most prominent creator of purely Utopian architectural fantasies among the Expressionists.[10]

Finsterlin's drawings, most of which date from between 1916 and 1923 – outstanding are the gaily coloured, gentle water colours – display a fantastic variety of organic forms reminiscent of Salvador Dali, a clear manifestation of its programmatic intent: the further evolution of the forms of the earth to create a second, artificial nature. Finsterlin was not much interested in function or construction; he was concerned with the primarily aesthetic vision of an "imaginary architecture", but behind its "humanity" lay the nightmares of Druillet. Characteristically the most frequent themes are isolated artists' studios or religious buildings; some of the early drawings are related to mythological subjects such as Atlantis.

But the protagonists of Expressionism were not only incorrigible dreamers in architecture. Bruno Taut moved from exuberant drawings to sober constructions, and his brother Max, four years younger, went through a similar development, as did Otto Bartning, three years younger than Bruno Taut, and Hans Scharoun, thirteen years his junior. Around the time of the First World War Max Taut was creating drawings of powerfully abstract vision, with an intensely mystical atmosphere emanating from the contrast between the dark shadows and the blinding light. The buildings he put up after the mid-1920s are remarkably factual. Otto Bartning alienated Gothic principles to elegant, sharply delineated graphics, which again have little in common with his later sober church buildings. Finally, even Hans Scharoun began with a dream architecture, forms striving dynamically upwards or unfolding crystalline structures already indicative of the latent organic tendency. But even in this youthful "Sturm und Drang" period the man who was later to be commissioned to rebuild Berlin and who was then one of the correspondents in the Gläserne Kette, was turning against the "botanical labyrinths" which Finsterlin, among others, was cultivating.

A similar development was that of Erich Mendelsohn, one of the major figures during the period of emotional tumult in architecture, who later also moved to a refined and bare style.[11] Generally referred to as an Expressionist, he never applied the term to himself, seeing in it an extreme which he rejected.

Nevertheless, the sketches which Mendelsohn, a cultural outsider, made between 1914 and 1917, and then supplemented with a new series after 1919, have an abstract and symbolic force of expression which is hard to surpass. The various themes – factory, observatory, corn silo, religious building – are always a pretext to research and bring out the dynamic inherent in the form. Almost exclusively in black and white, virtuoso drawings with broad strokes of the pen or charcoal, sheet upon sheet unfolding a stylistically uniform but fantastic world, the principle of unity of matter and energy discovered a few years previously – Mendelsohn was a personal friend of Einstein and had first-hand knowledge of the relativity theory – is given architectural expression. The influences of such different characters as Joseph Maria Olbrich (whom Mendelsohn greatly admired) and Antonio Sant'Elia are apparent, but they are combined into a completely independent language of boldly stressed horizontals, soft curves and supple forms. The dramatic movement which breaks out is given additional emphasis in the generally exaggerated perspectives with their immediate vanishing points. The "extroverted" internal force of the buildings gives expression to the "inner excitement of our time,"[12] which understandably left the young Mendelsohn, living and working in the Berlin of the twenties, utterly breathless.

But when he was building he kept a cool head. "The primary element is function", he said, although "function without sensibility remains mere construction."[13] Thus the Einsteinturm, which he built between 1917 and 1921 in Potsdam as a literal realisation of the architectural language of his sketches, remained unique: for his other buildings the former "young lion" chose a personal variant of the Rationalist aesthetic.

If Mendelsohn moved from a personal emotional exuberance into a factual and more relaxed future, the Amsterdam school, whose work overlaps in time with that of the Berlin architect, took exactly the reverse route: it came from a past of academic historicism to which it gave subjective intensification. Not for nothing did it draw mainly on the experience of Michel de Klerk and Pieter Lodewijk Kramer in designing the interior and details of Johan Melchior van der Mey's proto-Expressionist Scheepvaarthuis in Amsterdam (1911–16). In fact the drawings of the "Amsterdam chamber of horrors", as Werner Hegemann was later contemptuously to call it,[14] in their picturesque manner which mainly defines the overall form and "mood"

of a building, never entirely cast off a certain pedantic academicism. There are of course exceptions: the drawings by the gifted de Klerk, who quickly became the undisputed leader of the group, are fresh, innovative artistic statements combining formal elements from Hans Poelzig, Mario Chiattone and Erich Mendelsohn with echoes of traditional Dutch architecture as well as Art Nouveau into compositions of strong symbolic power and great force of expression.

More than almost any other architectural movement Expressionism was a feature of its age, limited in time, which soon burnt itself out. But again almost more than any other it was and is determined by the personalities of its protagonists, so that the short and short-lived paroxysm is overlaid by a coherence and continuity.

As a feature of its age Expressionism also carried with it architects who would not otherwise have been inclined to subjective expression or passionate outbreaks. Hans Poelzig, who had included emotional elements already in his very early sketches and buildings but otherwise remained bound to a correct traditionalism, created in several of his intensely visionary, often darkly mysterious projects some of the peaks of Expressionist architectural drawing, in which the dimension of fear determines lines and space. Hugo Häring forgot the programmatic functional links of his "organic building" and in 1922 produced in a competition for an office tower block on Friedrichstrasse in Berlin a drawing displaying a powerful and arbitrarily curved volume, presented, in analogy to many of Mendelsohn's sketches, in an exaggerated perspectivist approach which emphasises the dynamic mood. Strong strokes in charcoal and heavy shadows contribute to the tense, obscure atmosphere. Ludwig Mies van der Rohe, who shared his office with Häring for a time, had designed three years earlier a sharply-edged, pointed, fully glazed "crystal", whose rigor intensifies the aggressive movement. Here too the strongly perspectivist representation underlines the charged energy of the building, while the virtuoso use of charcoal explores the dialectics of reflection and transparency in the glass facade. Peter Behrens, whose professional and sure eclecticism was open to any stylistic influence, used a variant of Expressionism inspired by North German Brick Gothic in the administrative building he designed for the Hoechst-Aktiengesellschaft in Frankfurt am Main (1920–25), fixing its structurally determined force of expression in a series of charcoal perspectives.

As a movement borne by the personalities of its practitioners Expressionism lasted from the end of the nineteenth century (Karl Junker, for example, anticipated it in the house he built for himself in Lemgo in 1891–92) throughout the twentieth century. It found a wide variety of exponents: from Bruce Goff, a disciple of Frank Lloyd Wright, whose drawings are as eccentric as his buildings, reflecting in their compulsive search for novelty a misinterpreted artistic ideology of "innovation", through Gottfried Böhm, whose charcoal drawings may have been inspired by Hans Poelzig, Frei Otto with his huge Utopian light structures reminiscent of Bruno Taut's *Alpine Architektur* and designed to change whole landscapes, and Jørn Utzon with his deeply "emaciated" sketches reminiscent of Alvar Aalto's "journey through space and time" to Paolo Soleri with his links to mediaeval crafts and Peter Cook who has produced puzzling visions of a new Arcadia of sublimated passion, delicately sprayed in soft colours.

The Aesthetics of Reason:
From Tony Garnier to Richard Meier

Winner of the Prix de Rome in 1899 with a design for a bank building in the best Beaux-Arts tradition, Tony Garnier spent most of his time at the Académie de France in Rome not studying antiquity but designing the Cité Industrielle. The idea of architecture and urban design as one unity in the service of the modern industrial city was in itself innovative enough, at the beginning of the twentieth century: even more so the way in which the young Socialist solved his self-appointed task and presented it. The major part of the drawings published in Paris in 1917 as *Une Cité Industrielle, Etude pour la construction des villes* are concerned with the residential quarter, some with public buildings, and only very few actually show the industrial constructions that give the "brave new city" its name. What Garnier has shown in his plans and a series of precise, sharply drawn, in some cases coloured perspectives is a garden city with a rather high density. Its organisation anticipates the principles of rationalist urban planning while the design of the buildings demonstrates the consistent use of reinforced concrete, in those days a relatively new building material. The clarity and rationality of Garnier's presentation reflect the clarity and rationality of the concept. Certainly urban, constructional and technical innovations were to Garnier no reason to renounce classicism in the formal language of his city and its houses; that is evident not only from the sharply cut volumes and harmonic proportions but also in the constantly recurring antique fragments. Nevertheless, the dominant element is the use of logic and reason, apparent from the simplicity, sobriety and lack of ornamentation of the buildings. The detail of the representation is neither cajoling nor pedantic, it is the result solely of the need for both factual and illuminating communication: realism in the service of man. The drawings, of a very high quality, were first exhibited in 1904. Between 1906 and 1920 Garnier was able to realise a large number of his ideas in the Grands Travaux de la Ville de Lyon.

Ten years after the Cité Industrielle another vision of urban design was exhibited, this time influenced not so much by the English garden cities as by the new North American metropolises: the Città Nuova by Antonio Sant'Elia.[15] The drawings were shown together with works by his friend and partner Mario Chiattone in an exhibition of the group Nuove Tendenze. The catalogue contained a lively statement by Sant'Elia[16] proclaiming a new and revolutionary architecture. The text was revised a few months later by Filippo Tommaso Marinetti and published in the periodical *Lacerba* as "L'architettura futurista", thus establishing an – only partially conceptually justified – relationship between the Città Nuova and Italian Futurism.

Nevertheless, despite the loose ideological connection, Sant' Elia's urban visions are also affected by the cultural ambivalence of Futurism, hovering between revolutionary factuality and pathetic emotionalism. The trend at first appears to be severely rational and functionalist: the metropolis of the future is determined by the requirements of modern life, the main themes – the railway station, the electricity works, the residential tower blocks – come from the technical world or they are subordinate to it, the representation is clear, factual and reduced to the bare essentials. Still, the Città Nuova, on a closer examination, has undeniable romantic and irrational elements: "modern life", played out between bold, towering skyscrapers on huge streets with traffic routes crossing on

up to seven levels, is nothing else but the heroic mise en scène of the myth of speed and the machine; the technical functions of the buildings are given an aesthetic reinterpretation, often they are suppressed altogether, as the soaring structures, vaguely classified as "dinamismo architettonico", become quite functionless monuments to themselves; the drawing is no longer concerned to present a distanced and faithful image of the projected architecture and turns into the intense representation of its emotional and picturesque quality. Flat, rational perspectives composed of thin strokes drawn with a ruler in a relatively cold objectivity, contrast with expressive, supple drawings which with their powerful force, free lines and dramatic light and shade effects make no attempt to conceal their disturbing sensibility.

The Rationalist formal language had meanwhile penetrated far into progressive architectural circles in Europe. Auguste Perret combined the aesthetic compositional laws of the Beaux-Arts school with the technical conditions of working in reinforced concrete into a "new classicism" which found expression in delicate, severe drawings. Henri Sauvage, after a brilliant debut in the "organic" manner of Art Nouveau, developed parallel to this a simple, rectangular style whose influence on Sant'Elia is undeniable; he presented it in finely drawn black and white, an asceticism which, broken only by occasional ornament, forms a surprising contrast to the voluptuous, brightly coloured work of his "other half". Peter Behrens, who after his experience in the Munich Secession of 1893 moved first to Art Nouveau and then to classicism, found his way around 1907 to a moderate Rationalism; in his powerful perspectives classical and traditional elements remain essential components of the composition. Otto Wagner went through a radical change from historicism to a refined "modern style", proclaimed as early as 1894 in his inaugural lecture to the Vienna Academy, published a year later under the title *Moderne Architektur*. However, he took a deviant route around 1897 through the Vienna Secession which he generously supported and which was devoted to Art Nouveau. Much of his work after 1904 is characterised by horizontal lines, clear flat surfaces, right angles and pure forms.[17]

A particularly sharp break with the aesthetic tradition of the late nineteenth century was made by Adolf Loos. A great admirer of Otto Wagner, he opposed the irrational subjectivism and exquisite sensuality of the Vienna Secession with polemical bitterness. But for all his radicalism and desire for innovation he was not a revolutionary: even if he was far from following the fashionable Art Deco modernism of a Rob Mallet-Stevens, he was not prepared to give way to the subversive ethical and aesthetic imperatives of the Soviet Constructivist group around Vladimir Tatlin, Ivan Leonidov or El Lissitzky. After all he revered classical architecture and did not hesitate to use Doric columns or coffered ceilings in his own buildings and projects. The same attitude marks his drawings: with all their sparseness, an anti-aestheticism bordering almost on the terse, in some cases even the casual, they breathe, like Garnier's work, a classical spirit.

Walter Gropius in his early years was also characterised by a decided anti-aestheticism. His missionary didactic sense led him to concentrate more on communication than on the concrete realisation of architectural principles. Although the list of his works includes a number of remarkable buildings and projects, his main achievement was as catalyst, filter and crucible for the most progressive ideas of his time. The framework for this activity was the Bauhaus. First largely following the doctrine of William Morris, Gropius changed the direction of his school around 1922, mainly under the influence of De Stijl, giving less weight to the crafts and more to industrial design. The change, which was also affected by the economic situation in Europe and especially Germany, is reflected in Gropius' drawings: the neutral perfection of "machinist" representation cultivated by the protagonists of Neo-Plasticism affected his fruitful eclecticism too.

Very much more independent but by no means less complex in its borrowings and implications is the architectural work of Ludwig Mies van der Rohe. Like Loos a passionate admirer of Karl Friedrich Schinkel and like Jacobus Johannes Pieter Oud not uninfluenced by Hendrik Petrus Berlage and Frank Lloyd Wright, he took an active part in the Expressionist movement as director of the architectural programme of the Novembergruppe, edited for a short time the radical avant-garde periodical G, and maintained contact with the De Stijl group around 1922. From 1930 to 1933 he directed the Bauhaus and then from 1938 the School of Architecture of the Armour Institute (now the Illinois Institute) of Technology in Chicago. His stubborn statement that he was not interested in architectural style did not prevent him from borrowing both conceptually and stylistically during this eventful "éducation culturelle". But with all his receptivity to the most heterogeneous cultural influences his own architectural development remained of a consistency, coherence and conviction which have scarcely been equalled, and this was clearly due to the discipline and rationality with which he pursued his patient search, remaining awake and fresh even in his radicalism.

Mies van der Rohe's drawings[18] are a vivid testimony to the fact that logic and self-limitation need not produce rigidity. In a wide range of techniques, but preferably pencil and chalk, he explored the endless potential for expression of constructive and aesthetic elements reduced to the minimum, letting the surrounding and the light act on the aristocratic perfection of his forms and working through from the overall impression to the detail and from the detail back to the overall impression. Some of these sheets are rapid sketches, thrown quickly onto the paper and yet full of expression; others are complete drawings, generally perspectives. Some are mounted onto a photograph of the environment to give a realistic simulation. But everywhere the aim is apparent to reduce all the elements to their essentials and achieve that mythical essence in whose silence the order of a cryptic spiritual world is revealed.

In 1918, a year before Gropius founded the Bauhaus in Weimar, the first exhibition of Purism was held in Paris. In the catalogue Charles Edouard Jeanneret and Amédée Ozenfant published a manifesto with the significant title Après le Cubisme. After having declared offhand that Cubism was dead the authors proclaimed a new art which was to evolve from economy of means, collaboration with technology, and pure geometry. The exhibition showed schematic, bare compositions of simple objects, obviously disciplined to asceticism for the sake of an intellectual programme. The technique combined views and ground-plans in flat surfaces and was evocative of engineering drawings. Any kind of perspective was avoided.

But the doctrines of Après le Cubisme were only one stage in the development of a creative force which in its intense rationality and disciplined passion can be compared, in twentieth century art, only with that of Pablo Picasso. Both the passion and the rationality are manifest in the huge number of sketches and drawings which Le Corbusier, as Jeanneret

later called himself, has left together with a remarkable range of architectural work and a no less impressive list of publications and polemical writings.[19] Both the technique of the drawings and their trend vary continuously: some are in pencil, some in chalk, some in pen and ink. Some are laid out in colour but most are black and white with grey areas shaded in spots or oblique strokes. Some of the views are flat but the perspectives which were so despised during the "Purist" phase are now much more frequent. Some are in thin, exact lines, almost all are freehand, with courageous, powerful, imaginative strokes. The environment plays an important part in these architectural drawings, unlike in the radical work of De Stijl or Alberto Sartoris, from which it is banned; often the romantic exuberance of a broad landscape thick with trees, vaguely reminiscent of Frank Lloyd Wright, dominates the scene. But the emphatically artificial, Cartesian "objets trouvés" of the buildings always claim the most attention: they either stand out on distant hilltops, white against the sky, or shimmer in glass behind projecting branches, as the embodiment of the "jeu savant, correct et magnifique des volumes assemblés sous la lumière."[20] Le Corbusier's buildings take their place with a subtle poetry within nature, but do not stand in opposition to it.

The artistic contributions from Mies van der Rohe and Le Corbusier with their rational consistency and creative innovation stand out far above the general architectural culture of the twentieth century. But they were only possible on the humus of a rich intellectual and artistic environment. This included Hannes Meyer, whose realism, synthesized in the formula "architecture = function × economy", determines the hard edges and sharp lines of his terse drawings. It also included Ludwig Hilberseimer, who in the ruthless logic and icy coldness of his black and white axonometric work showed his contempt for any kind of subjectivity or "conciliatory gesture". Finally it included Marcel Breuer, whose perspectives seem gentle and expressive beside the severity of Hilberseimer's schematic presentations.

Two groups stand out from the general panorama and, with a little simplification, they can be placed one at the beginning and one at the end of the development of Rationalist architectural drawing in the first half of the twentieth century. Both fought under one and the same banner. They are the Dutch architects around the De Stijl movement and the Italian architects of the M.I.A.R. (Movimento Italiano per l'Architettura Razionale), and the common banner is axonometry.

Axonometry first appears in twentieth century painting in a work exhibited by Casimir Malevich in 1915 in Petrograd. It first appears in architectural drawing at a much later date, in 1923, in the De Stijl exhibition in the Paris gallery L'Effort Moderne.

The Neo-Plastic movement had already started in Holland in 1917 with the periodical De Stijl. The title of the magazine derives from Gottfried Semper's treatise Der Stil in den technischen und tektonischen Künsten. Jan Hessel de Groot, author of Vormharmonie and the theoretician behind Hendrik Petrus Berlage, shortened the name to De Stijl and so it remained. The name of the movement, however, was created by the painter Piet Mondrian. It refers to the central artistic intent to reduce the ideal structure of space (and hence consciousness) to the flat surface and express it in the proportional relations between areas limited by right angles and primary colours. The aim was to renounce the individual in favour of an objective and universal vision.

The same aim is manifest in the architectural drawings by the Neo-Plastic circle. One of the main features is the use of axonometry. This was reintroduced by Theo van Doesburg, the De Stijl spokesman, who brought about its theoretical integration with his basic principles of architecture.[21] It was adopted by the majority of the Rationalist architects of the twenties and became virtually the "leitmotiv" of the modern movement.

There are many reasons for the renunciation of perspective with vanishing points in favour of axonometry, and they are deeply rooted in the essence of Rationalist architecture. Van Doesburg stated in 1924: "The new architecture is *formless...*" It rejects schemes a priori and recognises neither symmetry nor frontality, instead it "offers the plastic richness of an all-sided development in space and time." (This implies a disposition to shift between the four dimensions of space and time.); "furthermore, the new architecture has rendered front, back, right, left, top, and bottom, factors of equal value."[22]

This explains already the inherent unsuitability of perspective drawing for the "new architecture". If architecture is no longer dependent on certain viewpoints but requires a multiple view taken from a range of always different points, and if these are programmatically removed from the front or from precisely fixed axes, it is no longer possible to place the viewer arbitrarily in *one* spot and expect him to perceive the building from there, as is the case in a perspective fiction. On the contrary, the building must be presented in as neutral a way as possible, the viewer should be free to choose his vantage point and be able to enjoy the innumerable and changing images of the object as he wishes.[23] Objectivity was the first reason for the preference given to axonometry by the Rationalists.

The second was economy. Axonometry achieves a uniquely synthetic presentation of architecture: two axonometries, taken from opposite corners, will give a comprehensive image of a design. Ground-plans, elevations and sections are all integrated; the dimensions can be read off directly from an isometrical ground-plan axonometry such as van Doesburg, for instance, preferred. The technique gives as comprehensive and precise information on the "objective" features of the real building as possible, so that all its aspects can be rationally comprehended. This is not the direct but partial view which a perspective will give, it is an indirect but total image, reduced to the smallest conceivable space.

The third reason was the desire for abstraction. The axonometric drawing simplifies the object it represents, and it does so by reducing it to precisely those elements which the Rationalists were particularly interested in: line, surface, volume, dimension. In doing so it pays more attention to the object than to the viewer, giving a precise image of the object but offering the viewer little assistance. The axonometric drawing is not so much a means to represent architecture as a working tool or even objectivised work. It gives priority to architectural production over architectural consumption and so it inevitably becomes a manifestation and a symbol of the increasing retreat of architectural culture into its specific disciplinary aspects and autonomous artistic essence.[24]

But despite these advantages axonometry did not come to be exclusively used. Both the Rationalists in the 1920s in general and the De Stijl group in particular continued to use perspective. Drawn with the utmost exactitude and carefully coloured, in the work of Jacobus Johannes Pieter Oud and Gerrit Thomas Rietveld perspective displays in an almost ostentatious perfection a language of forms removed from any naturalist model and oriented to an abstract technology. No human beings, trees or environmental elements contaminate the icy purism of the absolute objects. They themselves, houses not so much as abstract sculptures, are depicted with an extreme economy of means: straight lines and immaculate areas crossing and interpenetrating at right angles, the primary colours, red, blue and yellow, with white, black and grey as contrasts, the pure cube, not static and closed but dynamic, open, free of delimitation and part of endless space.

The "hard core" of the De Stijl group devoted themselves to abstraction and objectivity with a passionate and Calvinistic austerity. The unmistakable, essential elements in their work lie in the concept, not in the execution. It is not until the drawings of architects like Willem Marinus Dudok, who was influenced by De Stijl but followed Frank Lloyd Wright in developing an independent attitude, that "houses" characterised by an artistic subjectivity, even if a rather reserved one, are to be found again.

The poetic language of the Neo-Plastic movement has much in common with that of the Italian Rationalism of the 1920s and 1930s: not only the desire for purity, the need for abstraction and a tendency to radicalism, but first and foremost the longing for "clarity, revision and *order.*"[25]

This longing is very apparent in both the architecture and drawings of Giuseppe Terragni, who was strongly influenced by Le Corbusier, with whom he shared not only the Cartesian preference for elementary geometry but also the intellectual freshness. His persistent exploration of the Pythagorean, crystalline internal laws of architecture unfolds in clear drawings, some of which are touched in soft watercolour; for all their subtle classicism they do not deny the sensual dimension of the "architecture of reason".

Very much more abstract and even more strongly related to form "itself" are the purist axonometries and (much rarer) perspectives of Alberto Sartoris. The drawings, reduced to the absolute essence, are autonomous stages in that "search for the brilliance of geometry" which was for Sartoris a "constant of architectural creation."[26] Blindingly pure, abstract objects are presented in metaphysical isolation and enshrined in deep silence.[27]

In contrast to the sublime and on occasions moralising asceticism of Sartoris many of the European architects who took Rationalism to the United States displayed a tendency to aestheticism. The drawings by William Lescaze, with their borrowings from Art Deco, the dynamic vanishing point perspectives of Richard Neutra and the sophisticated coloured work of Rudolf Michael Schindler conceal behind a factual surface a frivolous, playful element.

This is an ambivalence which will recur after the Second World War in the willful pen-and-ink drawings of Paul Rudolph, whose initially appealing and characteristic "handwriting" was soon to degenerate into a fashionable stereotype. The draughtsmanship of Cesar Pelli is largely free of concessions of this kind, renouncing a strong visual impact to find its way back to a neutrality reminiscent of Mies van der Rohe's silence. Nevertheless, these ground-plans, views, sections and details, generally in pencil and sometimes shaded in grey, sometimes coloured, are not without an aesthetic ambition which lies in the American tradition of Hugh Ferris and his distinguished renderings. The same neutrality, this time free of manifest aesthetic claims, characterises the early drawings of James Stirling. The simple, sharply drawn black and white isometries are reminiscent of Sartoris, but with an elegant objectivity instead of his purist refinement. This was soon to be dropped for more varied experiments.

In these designs, however, the Rationalist techniques of representation of the 1920s and 1930s are still generally accepted and used; the search for novelty goes on within their borders. It is not until the American group known as the Five Architects[28] that these limits are overcome and the problems inherent in Rationalism are brought to a catharsis.

The purist special axonometries of Peter Eisenman, of the early Michael Graves, of Charles Gwathmey, of John Hejduk and of Richard Meier actually open up a completely new critical perspective with their extreme abstraction. Exactly through their inaccessibility and incomprehensibility they radically call in question the relation between architecture and its representation.[29] The fascinatingly complex work of Eisenman, in particular (whose 1980 house El Even Odd is an "axonometric object" that attempts to explore "the conditions of representation and reading in architecture"[30]), as well as the dream-like, poetic pieces of Hejduk (whose Diamond House of 1967 is not casually derived from the series of "compositions losangiques" by Piet Mondrian[31]) force the alienation of architecture from society, which was already apparent to van Doesburg, into a paroxysm. But by taking this to extremes, as they do for all their stupendously elegant and fully exploited virtuosity of draughtsmanship, they open the way to overcoming it.

Compared with such radicalism the works of Oswald Mathias Ungers or Rem Koolhaas (and his Office for Metropolitan Architecture) seem gentle and appealing: their cool axonometries take up again the myth of the modern movement, free it from the theoretical involutions of Eisenman or the cult-surrealist labyrinths of Hejduk and present it anew as a possible way out of a crisis which they are aware of but not greatly concerned about.

The Fascination of Technology:
From Richard Buckminster Fuller to Norman Foster

From out of the wide range of aesthetic, ideological and philosophical ideas and contradictions which survived from the nineteenth into the twentieth century, most of the architectural avant-garde of the 1920s chose Rationalism; they gave this a romantic intensification and sublimated it to the "aesthetics of reason". A smaller group, however, decided in favour of the more pragmatic components, split off and began to explore the possibilities of the direct transformation of technology into architecture without metaphoric "digressions".

All the "International" of the technological Utopia owe a debt to Richard Buckminster Fuller, who began consistently to develop technical "machines for living" as early as the 1920s. One of his creations is the Dymaxion House of 1927. His desire to achieve constructions which could be put up quickly and cheaply, cover as large an area and weigh as little as possible, led him not only to the development of the geodesic dome but also into the realm of urban Utopias. His drawings range from pleasing "handmade" sketches along the lines of strip cartoons to full technical drawings built on regular, seemingly endless repetitions of basic geometrical elements; these recall Victor Vasarely's experiments in Op Art and are of almost exactly the same period.

Fuller's ideas were taken up by Konrad Wachsmann, among others. Wachsmann was concerned not only to replace the slow, expensive and inefficient traditional methods of craft building by faster, cheaper and more efficient mass production, but also to develop modular construction systems which were to be both effective and aesthetically attractive. His drawings, to him not so much presentations as studies, in other words, essential stages in the design process, are not lacking in sensuality for all their filigree exactitude. Sometimes, indeed, representation and cropping are dominated by the dynamic released in the romantic Expressionist impetus of the Futurist visions.

A similar energy is apparent in the work of Kiyonori Kikutake, who was creating poetic Utopias of swimming cities as early as the 1950s; in 1961, together with Kisho Noriaki Kurokawa, Fumihiko Maki and Masato Otaka, he formed the Metabolist group. The group produced bold architectural and urban designs with fantastic and extreme but always logical forms of structural expression. These were an interpretation of the themes of constant growth and change and of the repeated interchange of units within one coherent organism, executed with a technical and expressive intensity.

In the same year as the Metabolist group another formation came into being in Great Britain, related to the Japanese team but much more legendary: Archigram. The group was founded by Peter Cook, Michael Webb and David Greene; they were later joined by Warren Chalk, Ron Herron and Dennis Crompton. The partners were bound by the belief that they were the intellectual heirs of the Futurists, indeed their direct heirs. They used the most advanced technical resources of the time, space capsules, robots and computers, and combined these into "buildings"; they designed the cities that every generation was supposed to build anew, thus applying the laws of the consumer society with a perfidious logic to architecture; they took "the beauty of movement" literally and actually went so far as to attach telescopic legs to their space-ship houses so that they could move from one place to another like a lunar module. Among their "heroes" were not only the Soviet Constructivists but also Dan Dare, Flash Gordon and Superman, a result of the group's craze for science fiction as well as of their proximity to Pop Art which had meantime, through the work of Roy Lichtenstein, begun to appreciate the aesthetic attraction of the strip cartoon.

The characteristic formal language of Archigram paradoxically derives its uniqueness from the radical exaggeration of technical impersonality. The metropolitan Utopias which have little hope of realisation unload their critical and intellectual potential already as works in an exhibition. Technically they all draw on the same repertoire: exact drawing, generally in black and white, always extremely precise and with the detail that could be expected of an engineering drawing, mostly flat views and sections, with the individual parts and elements named and numbered in thick stencilling. This is not simply to make the concept clearer: the lettering is an integral part of the graphic design, whose various elements are assembled as mechanistically as the "plug-in" and "clip-on" units of the mega-structures in the fictive reality. The "beautiful ugliness" of the virtuoso drawings matches that of the buildings they depict, which in their brusque honesty are clearly descended from the New Brutalism. But for all their exactitude and despite the cynicism which is apparent here and there the Archigram tableaux suggest the subtly cheerful throb of a beat festival in a Futurist metropolis. It is not by chance that many of the images in the Beatles cartoon film *Yellow Submarine* are not unlike those of Archigram.

Their "concrete" Utopias, a faithful and at the same time derisive picture of the 1960's unreflected belief in progress, provoked countless reactions, both critical and epigonal. Among the epigonal reactions are the organically composed visions of Günther Domenig and Eilfried Huth, as well as the elegant technical dreams of Stanley Tigerman. However, these have remained episodes in personal developments that should soon lead out of the preoccupation with architecture as technology.

Technology plays yet another role in the work of avant-garde didactic groups such as Haus-Rucker-Co or Coop Himmelblau, both rooted in the fermenting Vienna of Günther Feuerstein, Hans Hollein, Walter Pichler and Raimund Abraham. Technology here is, if not an arbitrary means, still a purely instrumental means to provoke the process of learning, an attempt to fulfill Herbert Marcuse's demand that art should "release the crippled unconscious and the crippled consciousness which strengthen the repressive establishment".[32] With all their differences the Haus-Rucker-Co team, founded in 1967 (Laurids Ortner, Günther Zamp-Kelp and Manfred Ortner) and the working partnership Coop Himmelblau, formed a year later (Wolf D. Prix and Helmut Swiczinsky) share the explicit intent to criticise, contradict and indicate alternatives not in the form of sane "ersatz" worlds but through aggressive drawings which make existing conflicts evident, if necessary with a brutal directness.

If Haus-Rucker-Co and Coop Himmelblau represent the idealist, "Action Art" aspect of technological architecture, the work of Norman Foster, Renzo Piano and Richard Rogers is its more pragmatic and above all more lasting expression: what the first two groups offer purely as a stimulus, in the form of a constant process, they develop up to more "finished" solutions.

Norman Foster looks back to Joseph Paxton, seeing architecture as primarily a technical problem. His drawings, which make no concession to and show no sign of an artistic pose even in their smallest detail, are purely factual. They are constructive and functional compositions. But out of this severe positivist discipline grows an architecture of skin and bone – the influence of Mies van der Rohe is obvious – revealing a subtle hint of classicism; the earlier pioneer's preference for nobility has given way to an asceticism which is no less refined for all its brusqueness.

The technological interpretation in the work of Renzo Piano is more aggressive. Like Cedric Price, who was intellectually near the Archigram circle in the 1960s, Piano sees social and political opportunities in the intelligent use of highly developed technology in building. His projects, carried out in intense dialogue with their users, are an attempt to honour the Metabolist vision of constant change.

Richard Rogers finally, who shared with Foster and Piano the experience of two office partnerships, uses a progressive technology in an attempt to achieve an "aesthetics of the building process". Piano and Rogers were able to realise their theoretical principles, but also the activist visions of the Futurists and Archigram, virtually to the letter in the Centre Pompidou in Paris (1971–77); even after more than sixty years the dreams of Antonio Sant'Elia had not lost their fascination and their power.

Nor had they lost their ability to be reinterpreted. In the monumental and transfigured creations of Ludwig Leo or the elegant scenic productions of Gustav Peichl it is less the anarchist than the idealist side of Sant'Elias's visions which has survived: the revolution is sublimated in aesthetics. Only the technical elements recall the cultural revolution which existing culture has meanwhile reabsorbed.

The Ambivalence of Tradition: From Heinrich Tessenow to Michael Graves

Throughout the twentieth century, in the shadow of the avantgarde, the cautious experiments of those architects who were concerned with a reform of building but could not bring themselves to give up their ties with tradition and expose themselves to the storms on the front line can be observed. Their reserved attitude, oscillating between circumspection and reaction, is reflected in drawings which, while not denying their origin in the Romantic Picturesque school, move beyond this – though to different extent and with varying success.

The rejection of the abstraction which the Rationalists of the 1920s and 1930s, for example, had propounded, is apparent already in the early pen-and-ink drawings by Theodor Fischer, as elegant as they are controlled, or Paul Bonatz. With all their underlying emotion these works have little in common with the sensual exuberance of the Expressionist representations. They are precise perspectives, balanced on a conservative line technique which almost always succeeds in avoiding conventional academicism.

That the balance is precarious can be seen in a comparison with the incomparably more independent and personal drawings of Heinrich Tessenow.[33] Tessenow, too, used mainly pen and ink and he too – a Biedermeier self-restraint – avoided colour; he too gave preference to perspectives and too sought the naturalist image. But he developed a style whose individuality and power are hard to match. In his early drawings Tessenow was still using the light lines and a graphic lay-out derived from Art Nouveau, but he soon moved away from any model to produce in fine, short strokes, distributed with the utmost parsimony on the paper, enchanting visions of a simple architecture. In an exact counterpart of his approach to life as well as to architecture, the balanced compositions, like the terse forms of his buildings, are comprised of a few constantly recurring elements and of omissions, a silence blossoming into multiple significance under the gaze of the observer. As in Tessenow's architecture, this is order without dogmatism, typification without mechanisticism, classicism without patheticism. It is precisely in his stubborn rejection of innovation for its own sake that Tessenow achieves a dimension of newness which is of duration and free of any fashionable touch.

After such inimitable (but of course often imitated) quality, the coarsely expressive perspectives of Marcello Piacentini or the finer linear drawings of Erik Gunnar Asplund are a step down: they lack the freshness which can only come into being when the artist is not striving for tradition but stands firmly and easily in it because he has never attempted to separate from it.

This may well be said of Auguste Perret, whose neo-classical creations are presented in a bold and dynamic bird's-eye view often reminiscent of Tony Garnier, but also not without the echoes of some of the more adventurous perspective work of the Soviet Constructivists. The same applies to Eliel Saarinen and Ely Jacques Kahn, although their intentions and cultural background were quite different. Their dramatic renderings in pencil and charcoal are a striking illustration of the American longing for history: powerful forms which move between Art Deco and historicism. Hugh Ferris' early experiments[34] with massive volumes, mysterious shadows and dramatic light arrangements live on in almost Expressionist visions, monumental materialisations before disconcertingly stormy skies.

14

A similar style to that of Perret is recognisable in Wilhelm Kreis, whose early exuberance gave way in the 1930s to an elegant but academic neo-classicism. On the other hand, the techniques and "moods" of American architectural mises en scène of the period around the 1929 slump were incorporated by Philip Johnson after the Second World War into a refined eclecticism and taken to an almost oppressing perfection. But in these exquisite drawings the light-hearted, superficial charm of Francis Scott Fitzgerald's Jazz Age has fled, leaving a yawning disillusionment, a disenchanted emptiness whose intelligent cynicism keeps hiding behind ever new and increasingly refined masks from the past.

Cynicism, masks, the past – these are also the main elements in Robert Venturi's philological explorations in architecture. But he adds something else, a combination of seriousness and playfulness. A light touch, which Venturi seems to feel is necessary and derives, in a seeming paradox, from the far-reaching, at times even meticulous analysis of the problems of architecture in the present pluralist consumer society, also characterises his projects as well as his drawings. In endless delight in experiment he probes the possibilities of a huge range of techniques and methods; adventuring above all into current advertising techniques including poster collage and strip cartoons.

A comparable approach is apparent in Charles Moore's work, although in representing his eclectic regionalist projects he is more inclined to sacrifice the pleasure of experiment to the certainty of the experimented. Most of his drawings are naturalist vignettes, transmitting the illusion of the finished building in its intended context as realistically as possible. More free, if again not entirely without concessions to popular taste, is the graphic work of Robert Stern[35] and Stanley Tigerman; both never renounce the claim to autonomous art, even if this entails sacrificing some ability to communicate. Thus, so to speak, through the back door, abstraction (and with it, of course, axonometry) enters the concrete repertoire of traditionalist architectural drawing.

The situation is different with Michael Graves,[36] the most willful exponent in the American group around Venturi. After a brilliant debut with the neo-Rationalist Five Architects he was strongly influenced by Venturi's mannerism, but he did not yield to his populist tendency; so he developed into an independent painter-architect, probing the volumetric compositional laws of architecture in elegant, slim sketches and unfolding an iconography of classical set pieces and ruins in virtuoso tableaux. For Graves architectural drawings are "tangible speculations", which may be made to a specific intent but then quickly develop a life of their own that in its turn exercises a decisive influence on the architectural product. He uses a wide range of techniques, most of them derived from painting; colour plays a major part, imparting a strangely disturbing, melancholic and autumnal mood to the monumental remains of a past which cannot be revived, however many efforts are made. The tones recall the Romantic shadows and the nuances of Viennese "fin de siècle" and indirectly, therefore, the drawings of Walter Pichler, some of those by Hans Hollein and, if only faintly, the alienated compositions of Friedrich St. Florian.

Apart from the common acknowledgment of tradition in the widest possible sense, nothing could be further from the decadent and over-refined excesses of the disillusioned Graves than the powerful craftsmanship of Mario Ridolfi. There is not only a generation but a whole world between them: for Ridolfi

is rooted in the optimistic political mood of Italian Neo-Realism and the regional culture of suburban Rome and its surrounds. His drawings are not those of an architect but an "artigiano", an artisan – realistic, clear, full-blooded, rough, ground-plans, elevations and sections thrown down in self-confident carelessness all on the same sheet of paper, briskly filled with dimensions and lettered. Even orientation lines, passing marginal sketches and test strokes are part of the design; the concern is not with presentation, since these are nothing but working tools, even more: it is materialised work.

The sheets by Paolo Portoghesi[37] have the same rudimentary, almost brusque character, but the tool has become a work of draughtsmanship which does not deny that its function is to represent what is to be built (and not, as Ridolfi's work does, to aid the building process). The same is even more apparent in several of the drawings produced by James Stirling during his transitional phase from Rationalism to a radical eclecticism, as well as in many of the drawings by Ricardo Bofill and his Taller de Arquitectura[38]: the rough and unfinished becomes a pose.

Towards a New Autonomy:
From Louis Kahn to Aldo Rossi

After the mid-1950s in international architectural culture a reaction set in to much of what had been taken over from the avant-garde of the 1920s and 1930s in the post-war years. Anti-historicism was countered with a stronger inclination to reflect on history, anti-formalism (which had mainly been theoretical anyway) with a new attention to the architectural form, the inter-disciplinary trend with a renewed emphasis on the independence and autonomy of architecture.

Hand in hand with this "self-absorption" came a major revaluation of architectural drawing as a specific discipline. For an architecture which is capable of living in itself the drawing is the best means of tracing the essence of this "life", and with the renewed artistic claim greater attention to graphic art again becomes a legitimate preoccupation. At first hesitantly, then with more self-confidence and meanwhile in hectic enthusiasm the representation of architecture has moved back into the focus of attention of producers, consumers and critics.

The figurehead in the contradictory process of re-establishing architecture with a capital "A" was played by Louis Kahn; trained in the classical Beaux-Arts tradition, he fought all his life and throughout his work with latent or (later) explicit recourse to history against the "loss of the centre" deplored by Hans Sedlmayr. His – deeply American – longing for the immutable principles of a powerful tradition finds particularly forceful expression in his drawings which evoke primary forms and types of architecture with intense, obstinate strokes. Generally freehand, often rapidly sketched and frequently unfinished, Kahn's perspectives are vivid witnesses to his creative drive. He certainly does not draw back from graphic imperfection, not even from clumsiness: for all their inescapable attraction these drawings are not a means of presentation, they are stages on the way to building. It is this unmistakable purpose which gives them their unusual power.

James Stirling's sketches have a striking similarity to those by Kahn: the same handling of line, the same plasticity and suppleness, the same objectivised search through a constant change of single elements and their relations, the same unleashed, unbroken energy. The energy is also manifest in the final drawings, but here it is softened by an almost smooth perfection, the earlier black and white perspectives (some of which were executed by Leon Krier) in fine, exact strokes, the latest more complicated axonometric representations, difficult to unravel, which are generally willfully coloured in crayon. The surprising and confusing radical eclecticism which characterises Stirling's architecture, so rich in twists and turns but consistent even in these twists and turns, also reflects in his drawings.

The same may be said of the work of Arata Isozaki, who moves with remarkable brilliance (and equally remarkable nonchalance) from one architectural trend to another, trying out virtually every technique of representation. The early rigorous axonometric black and white drawings are reminiscent of those of the Five Architects, without emulating their intellectual involutions and artistic balancing acts. Gradually the initial self-restraint has given way to a delight in experiment which is as elegant as it is mannered.

A very different intellectual and artistic discipline moves through the work of Josef Paul Kleihues. His "poetic Rationalism" takes form in drawings of a simplicity which is not spontaneous but the result of an intense process of purification. Precisely drawn in pen and ink and coloured in crayon, flat elevations on brown packing paper take architectural drawing back beyond spectacular effect to its elementary typology, without renouncing the vividness and craftsmanship of drawing itself. Finedly reduced isometries illustrate the three-dimensional geometric compositional laws of the projects. Simple perspectives, generally in black and white, discretely reproduce the spatial impression. Architectural drawing is again a means to an end without giving up its sensuous quality.

An analogous reduction and refinement is apparent in the graphic work of Oswald Mathias Ungers: but where Kleihues keeps trying out new methods of presentation while preserving his personal style, Ungers dresses virtually all of his (remarkably variant) projects in the same way: an elegant, linear, quite technical axonometry, which does not, as it does, for instance, for the Five Architects, serve primarily as a means to abstraction, but first and foremost to illuminate the spatial composition and the construction. Ungers' drawings, whether black and white or coloured, are always full of exact detail, they are extremely clear and densely packed: they leave no item of information out which it is possible to provide within the framework of the particular representation and its scale.

Although there are some philosophical and methodological similarities, it would be hard to imagine a greater contrast to Ungers' self-obligation to clarity than Rob Krier's longing for concealment: in all the sketches and drawings by the Luxembourg architect the element of cover, of what is latent and not yet brought to the surface, plays a central role.[39] Regardless of whether these are "free" studies or architectural designs, and regardless of whether the designs are views, perspectives or axonometries (generally with ground-plans projected on to the roof surface): again and again the theme of the mask is to be found. The strong, free-hand strokes, the shadows, the powerful colours and even the hand-written comments, all underline the craftsmanship and deep-rooted emotionality reflected in a virtuoso evocation of melancholical monumental images.

In comparison, the work of Rob's younger brother Leon is cooler and more controlled: if Rob is the architect of reasonable passion, Leon is the master constructor of passionate

reason.[40] Here, too, there are rapid and virtuoso strokes of the pen, harmonious colours, old techniques carried on almost to affectation; here, too, refinement of detail, grandiose perspectives, romantic and picturesque "vedutas". But instead of Rob's extrovert exuberance this is a considered economy and logical stringency. The archaeology of classicism is pursued with an industrious and systematic consistency, without melancholy and certainly not in resignation. At most there is a hint of nostalgia. But only a hint: for the certainty of being rooted in a tradition whose continuity lies outside history and remains independent of temporary phenomena or episodes, allows Krier to evoke his visions, which may in many ways seem anachronistic, with serene ease. He is not working for this society but for a (self-created) ideal.

A similar idealism characterises the bravura pieces of drawing by Raimund Abraham.[41] However, while Krier moves back to the tradition of pre-industrial age which he transfigures into an Arcadia, Abraham stands quite still: like Tessenow, he has never moved away from tradition per se. The subtly harmonising earth colours of his magically alienated axonometries radiate in an empty space in which there is no life and no time. Only the quintessence of architectural poetry is omnipresent in the metaphysical crystallisations.

Even further from concrete realisation, even more extremely metaphoric are the confusingly labyrinthine graphics by Daniel Libeskind[42], who has reinterpreted Piranesi's frightening visions of destruction, or the refined water-colours and oil paintings by Massimo Scolari[43], highly individual interpretations of the theme of silence, unyielding compositions of an icy beauty. Here, as in the paintings by Arduino Cantafora[44], architectural drawing reaches a peak of expression and autonomy; but at the same time of desperate protest.

A protest which, far less despairing and with varying intensity, can be found in almost all the drawings of the current architectural avant-garde: in the dry axonometries of Giuseppe Grossi and Bruno Minardi[45], who are playing an ambiguous game with abstract representations in nostalgic guise; in the metaphysical alienated work by Diana Agrest and Mario Gandelsonas, who present the metamorphoses of the modern movement with enigmatical irony; in the elegant perspectives by Rodolfo Machado and Jorge Silvetti, embodying a more philological combination of modernism and tradition; in the perfect pen and ink drawings by Franco Purini[46], most of which compensate for the complexity of their technique and the range of their signs by leaving out all colour and using only black and white; in the refined graphic compositions of Bruno Reichlin and Fabio Reinhart, who often use a spray technique, combining different elements of one plan on the same sheet of paper in cryptic ambiguity; in the extremely abstract axonometries of Mario Botta[47], in which drawing virtually renounces its primary function to inform, and, like the architecture which it is actually supposed to represent, becomes a symbol of itself; finally in the perspectives of Vittorio Gregotti, both simple and charming, which combine rational discipline with picturesque appeal in a quiet and unobtrusive way.

To an even greater extent than for most of these architects the graphic work of Giorgio Grassi[48] is not merely an illustration but an essential and inseparable element of his design work: the drawings are stages in a reduction which, according to Grassi, is the only way to a collective language in a pluralist society. The elementary, crystalline quality of the precise and fine strokes, stark forms and delicate colours – although colour is rare – is an exact reflection of the quality of the envisaged architecture: its contours, volumes, spaces and aura. Both the rigour of the drawing and that of the concept are products of an intense intellectual and artistic process, which aims to meet Georg Lukács' demand for aesthetic realism through a deliberate self-limitation. The result is a subtly neutral, "objective" abstraction, which is not enjoyable at superficial glance. It is only on a second viewing that the harmonious, mathematical network, reduced to the ideal essence, becomes apparent. Each individual can breathe into this "open" emptiness the questions which move him, his hopes and his fears, and listen to the enigmatical echo of his own dreams.

The same openness can be observed in the drawings by Aldo Rossi[49], who casts a shadow over virtually the whole of present-day avant-garde architectural culture. Rossi began his obsessive search for the "truth" theoretically in his first writings of 1956, and in practice with his first projects of 1962. Gradually he developed, on the basis of a severe Rationalism, a systematic theoretical construction which lays down the compositional laws of architecture in the best tradition of enlightenment and delimits its disciplinary core as an independent science outside any form of historical relativism. His drawings are a particularly clear distillation of the "leitmotiv" (and the peculiarity) of his work. In a wide range of media and techniques they are all exploring but one thing: the possibility of combining a handful of elementary forms, archetypal elements which make up the repertoire of architecture per se. The general and the generally applicable are combined with autobiographical motifs, and these in turn are sublimated to abstract emblems through reduction and repetition.

Even if a disenchanted glance over the chaos of a new "epoch of the crisis"[50] inevitably must confirm that "now this is lost,"[51] the classical order of things has irretrievably collapsed, for Rossi this is still no cause for resignation. With every drawing the long wearisome process "to create order out of the desperate confusion of our time"[52] starts with renewed determination. And from zero: for the yearned-for logic is not searched out in what is already existing; it is implanted afresh into the chaos with each "new" object. In a world of fragments any attempt to create structures of a total order is bound to fail; only new fragments, the seeds of a future logic, will be able to provoke some changes in reality.

That is also the underlying reason for Rossi's untiring, ceaseless production of drawings, always evoking the same in ever new arrangements: the hope of hammering order into a cosmos to which it is apparently totally alien. How thin the thread of the hope is can be seen from the not very serene atmosphere of the metaphysical constructions behind whose rationality the bottomless horror of Expressionism occasionally flares up. But however thin it may be, the hope is there. The "confusion of our time" is "desperate", but the despair does not infect those who have come to struggle against it with their ideas, their buildings and their images. That may not be much; but "we want no more; we can do no more."[53]

In Organic Architecture then, it is quite impossible to consider the building as one thing, its furnishings another and its setting and environment still another. The Spirit in which these buildings are conceived sees all these together at work as one thing. All are to be studiously foreseen and provided for in the nature of the structure. ...

To thus make of a human dwelling-place a complete work of art, in itself expressive and beautiful, intimately related to modern life and fit to live in, lending itself more freely and suitably to the individual needs of the dwellers as itself an harmonious entity, fitting in color, pattern and nature the utilities and be really an expression of them in character, – this is the tall modern American opportunity in Architecture.

Frank Lloyd Wright, 1910[1]

In organic architecture, any conception of any building as a building begins at the beginning and goes *forward* to incidental expression as a picture and does not begin with some incidental expression as a picture and go groping *backward*. This is modern.

Eye-weary of reiterated bald commonplaces wherein light is rejected from blank surfaces or fallen dismally into holes cut in them, organic architecture brings the man once more face to face with nature's play of shade and depth of shadow seeing fresh vistas of native creative human thought and native feeling presented to his imagination for consideration. This is modern.

The sense of interior space as reality in organic architecture coordinates with the enlarged means of modern materials. The building is now found in this sense of interior space; the enclosure is no longer found in terms of mere roof or walls but as "screened"–space. This reality is modern.

In true modern architecture, therefore, the sense of surface and mass disappears in light, or fabrications that combine it with strength. And this fabrication is no less the expression of principle as power-directed-toward-purpose than may be seen in any modern appliance or utensil machine. But modern architecture affirms the higher human sensibility of the sunlit space. Organic buildings are the strength and lightness of the spiders' spinning, buildings qualified by light, bred by native character to environment–married to the ground. That is modern!

Frank Lloyd Wright, 1930[2]

It still seems to many people inconceivable that a house too may be evolved entirely as an "organic structure", that it may be "bred" out of the "form arising out of work performance", in other words that the house may be looked upon as "man's second skin" and hence as a bodily organ. And yet this development seems inescapable. A new technology, working with light constructions, elastic and malleable building materials, will no longer demand a rectangular house, but permit or put into effect all shapes that make the house into a "housing organ". The gradual structural shift from the geometrical to the organic, which is taking place throughout our whole spiritual life and to some extent has already taken place, has made the form of work performance mobile as opposed to geometrical. The need to create form constantly leads the artist to experiment with styles, repeatedly leads him, in the interest

of expression, to spread shapes over objects – whereas the form arising out of work performance leads to every object receiving and retaining its own essential shape. The artist stands in the most essential contradiction to the form of work performance so long as he refuses to give up his individuality; for in operating with the form arising out of work performance the artist is no longer concerned with the expression of his own individuality but with the expression of the essence of as perfect as possible a utilitarian object. All "individuals" – and the stronger they are as personalities, and at times the louder they are, the more this applies – are an obstacle in the path of development, and in fact progress takes place in spite of them. But nor does progress take place without them, without individuals, artists and strong personalities. ...

This work begins where the engineer, the technologist, leaves off; it begins when the work is given life. Life is not given to the work by fashioning the object, the building, according to a viewpoint alien to it, but by awakening, fostering, and cultivating the essential form enclosed within it.

Hugo Häring, 1932[3]

Nature, biology, offers profuse and luxuriant forms; with the same constructions, same tissues and same cellular structures it can produce millions and millions of combinations, each of which is an example of a high level of form. Human life comes from the same roots. The objects that surround man are hardly mere fetishes and allegories with some mystical eternal value. They are more likely to be cells and tissues, alive just as cells and tissues are, the building components of which human life is composed. They cannot be dealt with in a different way from biology's other units, otherwise they would be in danger of becoming unsuited to the system, of becoming inhuman. ...

We have admitted, and probably agree, that objects which can with justification be called "rational" often suffer from a considerable lack of human quality.

Alvar Aalto, 1935[4]

In contrast to the view which sees in established forms and the standardization of new forms the only way towards architectural harmony and a building technology that can be successfully controlled, I ... want to underline that the most profound property of architecture is a variety and growth reminiscent of natural organic life. I should like to say that in the end this is the only real architectural style. If barriers are set up before it, architecture fades and dies.

Alvar Aalto, 1938[5]

After all, nature is a symbol of freedom. Sometimes nature actually gives rise to and maintains the idea of freedom. If we base our technical plans primarily on nature we have a chance to ensure that the course of development is once again in a direction in which our everyday work and all its forms will increase freedom rather than decrease it.

Alvar Aalto, 1949[6]

1 Frank Lloyd Wright 1905

2 Frank Lloyd Wright 1906

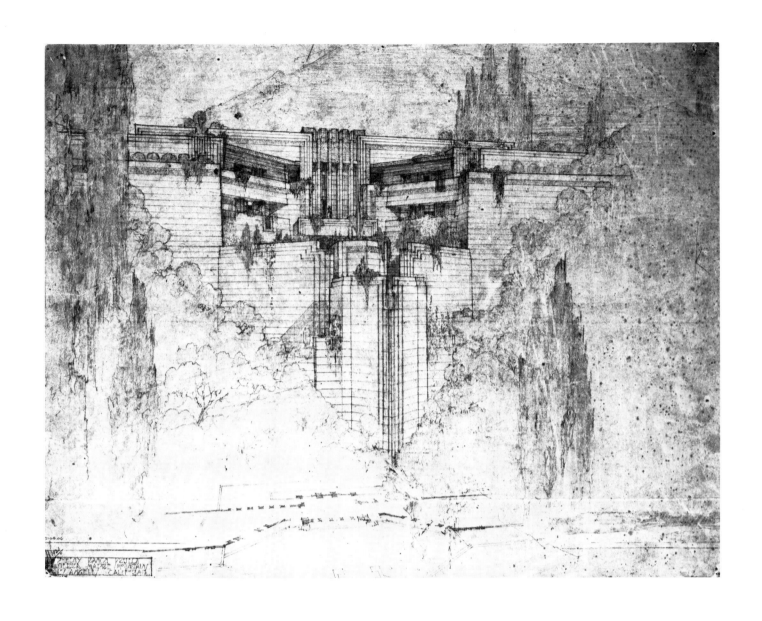

3 Frank Lloyd Wright 1921

4 Frank Lloyd Wright 1925

5 Frank Lloyd Wright 1929

BEBAUUNG der PRINZ ALBRECHT GÄRTEN

6 Hugo Häring 1924

GUT GARKAU

7 Hugo Häring 1924

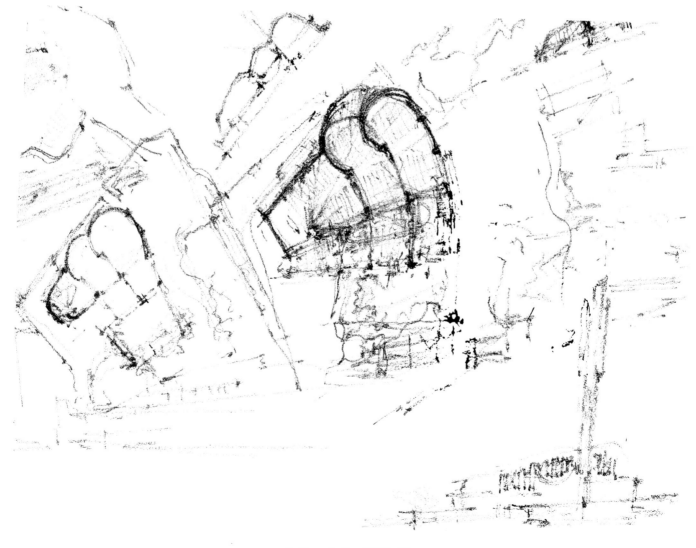

8 Alvar Aalto (1956–58)

9 Alvar Aalto 1958

10 Alvar Aalto (1962–64)

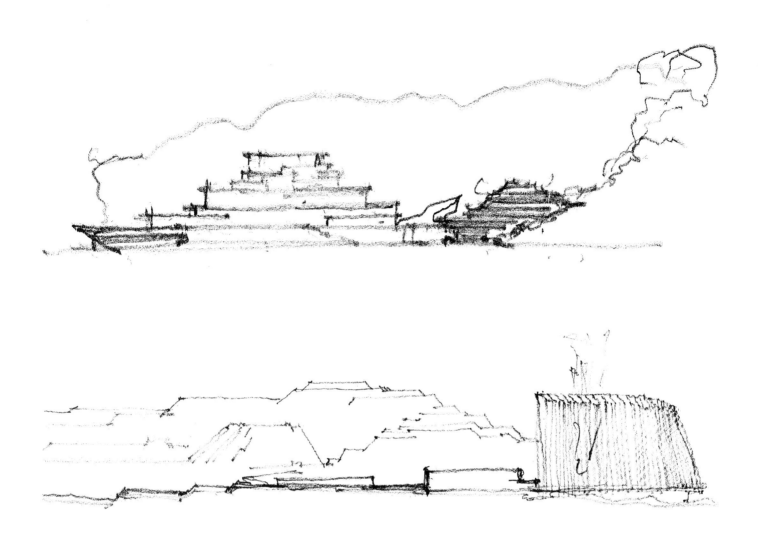

11+12 Alvar Aalto 1958

13 Eero Saarinen (1953)

14 Le Corbusier 1951

What is architecture? The crystalline expression of man's noblest thoughts, his ardour, his humanity, his faith, his religion! That is what it once *was*! But who of those living in our age that is cursed with practicality still comprehends its all-embracing, soul-giving nature? We walk through our streets and cities and do not howl with shame at such deserts of ugliness! Let us be quite clear: these grey, hollow, spiritless mock-ups, in which we live and work, will be shameful evidence for posterity of the spiritual descent into hell of our generation, which forgot that great, *unique* art: *architecture*. ... Structures created by practical requirements and necessity do not satisfy the longing for a world of beauty built anew from the bottom up, for the rebirth of that spiritual unity which ascended to the miracle of the Gothic cathedrals. We shall not live to see it. But there is one consolation for us: the *idea,* the building up of an ardent, bold, forward-looking architectural idea to be fulfilled by a happier age that must come. Artists, let us at last break down the walls erected by our deforming academic training between the "arts" *and all of us become builders again!* Let us together will, think out, create the new idea of architecture. Painters and sculptors, break through the barriers to architecture and become fellow builders, fellow strugglers for the final goal of art: the creative conception of the cathedral of the future, which will once again be all in *one* shape, architecture and sculpture and painting.

Walter Gropius, 1919[7]

—"Oh, our concepts: space, home, style!" Ugh, how these concepts stink! Destroy them, put an end to them! Let nothing remain! Chase away their schools, let the professorial wigs fly, we'll play catch with them. Blast, blast! Let the dusty, matted, gummed up world of concepts, ideologies and systems feel our cold north wind! Death to the concept-lice! Death to everything stuffy! Death to everything called title, dignity, authority! Down with everything serious! ...
In the distance shines our tomorrow. Hurray, three times hurray for our kingdom without force! Hurray for the transparent, the clear! Hurray for purity! Hurray for crystal! Hurray and again hurray for the fluid, the graceful, the angular, the sparkling, the flashing, the light — hurray for everlasting architecture!

Bruno Taut, 1920[8]

As creators ourselves we know how very variously the forces of motion, the play of tensions, work out in individual instances. All the more, then, is it our task to oppose excited flurry with contemplation, exaggeration with simplicity, uncertainty with a clear law; to rediscover the elements of energy in the midst of the fragmentation of energy, from the elements of energy to form a new whole. To work, construct, re-calculate the Earth! But *form* the world that is waiting for you. Form with the dynamics of your blood the functions of its reality, elevate its functions to dynamic supra-sensuality. Simple and certain as the machine, clear and bold as construction. From real presuppositions form art, from mass and light form intangible space.

Erich Mendelsohn, 1923[9]

Awake! Awake from the compulsive sleep into which you children of Adam have been plunged by the unripe fruit of the world tree and pluck your divine happiness, now never to be lost again, from its infinite branches: the knowledge of the primal meaning of all being – "development". ...
I beg you to lay aside the illusion that the purpose of human building is to create dwelling-places, that is to say sheltering caverns, for objects, plants, animals, men, and gods. All predetermined purpose falls like a heavy, inhibiting hand upon the motive force of a divinely free, pure will. ...
Building is the experience of space; inspiration, invention, the clearest, most sudden awareness of the soul's echo in the primeval jungle of the environment; a purposeless, unexampled play of the finest forces in porous matter whose flux came to a standstill in a moment of highest reflection, oblivious of pleasure, existing in appearance only, a waking sleep of forces, a *stationary movement* that might at any time continue to flower in all directions or disintegrate into well-shaped component parts, spontaneously splitting up like a living crystal without beginning or end like everything through which there quivers the pulse of the eternal.

Hermann Finsterlin, 1924[10]

We want no inhibitions and checks by recipes, we want the free spirit to find its own laws. The creative moment demands not the transparent wall, not the beautiful surface, not construction but synthesis. And this synthesis is not the sum of petty and doubtful details, but the outcome of an intuitive frenzy.
... We do not wish to renounce the factors that increase our feeling for life and the world. We want to experience the intoxication of our blood in all things...
We want the individual room, not the factory-made product; we want personality, not norm, not schema, not series, not type. We want no violation of our creative feeling, not even by architecture, we want to live our life. The wealth of the spirit shall glow, all productive possibilities shall blossom, unconcerned about "objectivity". Give form to the inner vigour, that cold souls may become warm.

Bernhard Hoetger, 1928[11]

"Modern functionalism" in architecture is dead. In so far as the "function" was a survival – without even an examination of the Kingdom of the Body upon which it rested – it came to grief and was exhausted in the mystique hygiene + aestheticism. (The Bauhaus, Le Corbusier's system, etc.) ...
I oppose to the mysticism of Hygiene, which is the superstition of "Functional Architecture", the realities of a Magical Architecture rooted in the totality of the human being, and not in the blessed or accursed parts of this being.

Frederick Kiesler, 1947[12]

SCHNEE
GLETSCHER
GLAS

Firnen
im ewigen Eise
und Schnee ~
überbaut und ge-
schmückt mit
Umbauungen, Flä-
chen und Blöcken
von farbigem Glase
– Bergblüten –

Die Ausführung ist gewiss ungeheuer schwer und opfervoll, aber nicht unmöglich. „Man verlangt so selten
von den Menschen das Unmögliche" (Goethe)

15 Bruno Taut (1917–19)

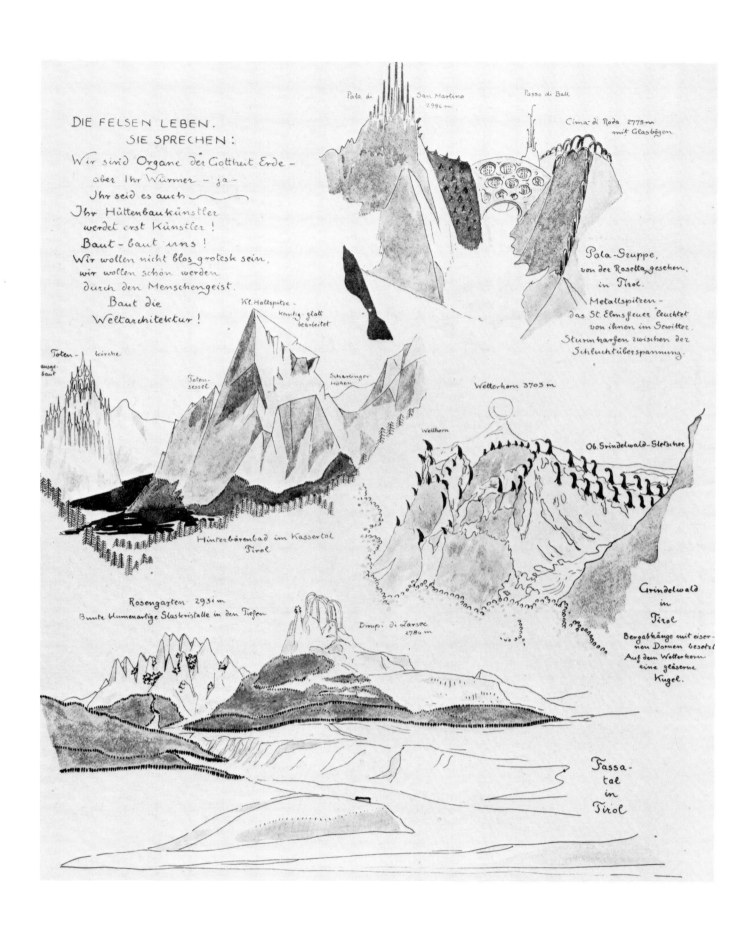

16 Bruno Taut (1917–19)

34

DOMSTERN

17 Bruno Taut (1917–19)

18 Hans Scharoun 1920

19 Wenzel August Hablik 1921

20 Otto Bartning 1921

21 Max Taut 1921

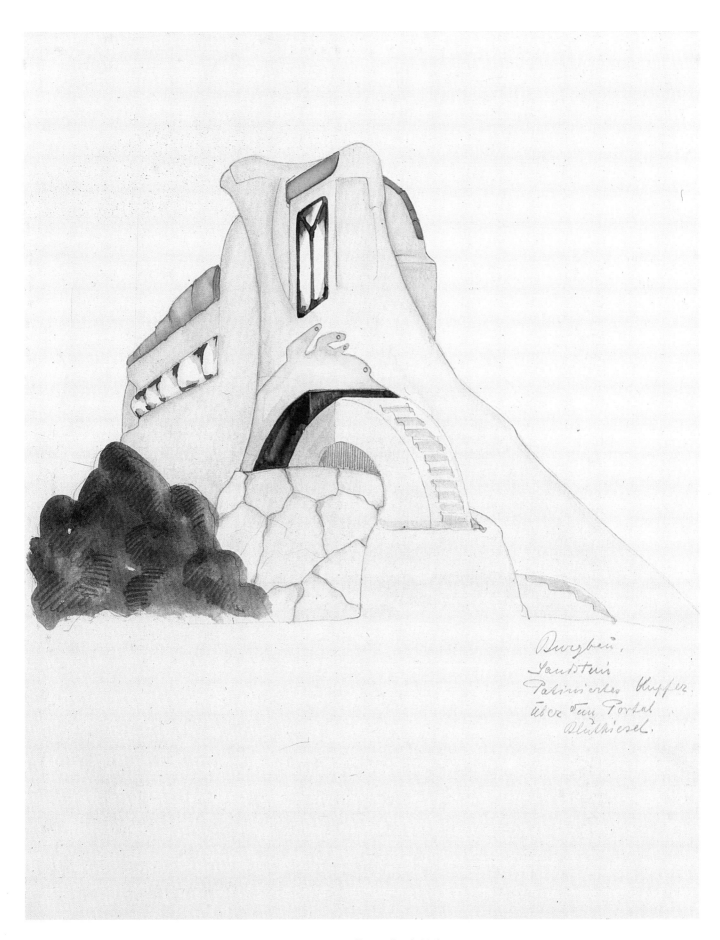

22 Hermann Finsterlin (1920)

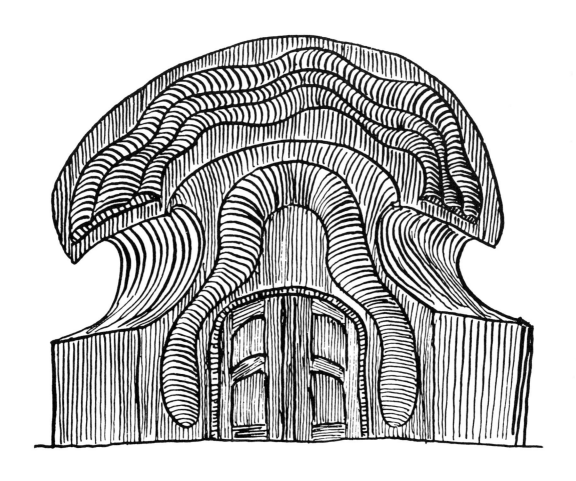

23 Paul Gösch (1920)

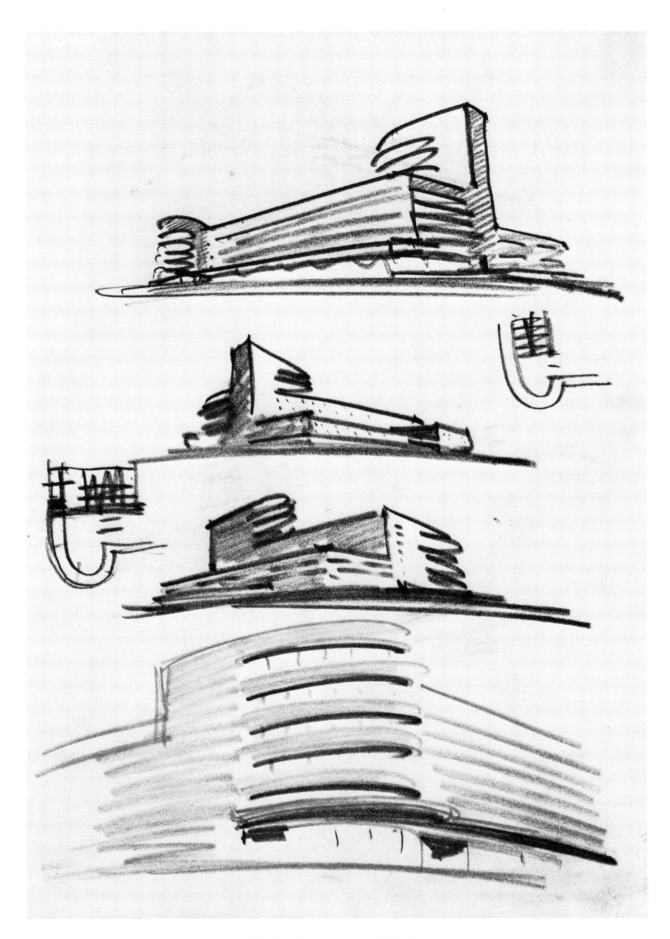

24 Erich Mendelsohn (1926–28)

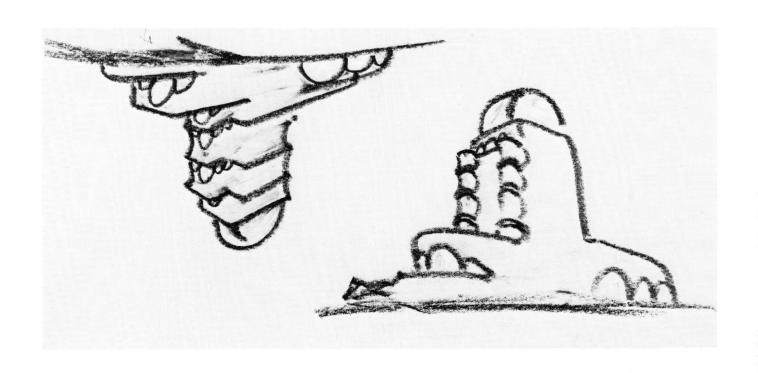

25 Erich Mendelsohn 1920

26 Rudolf Steiner, Carl Schmid-Curtius 1913

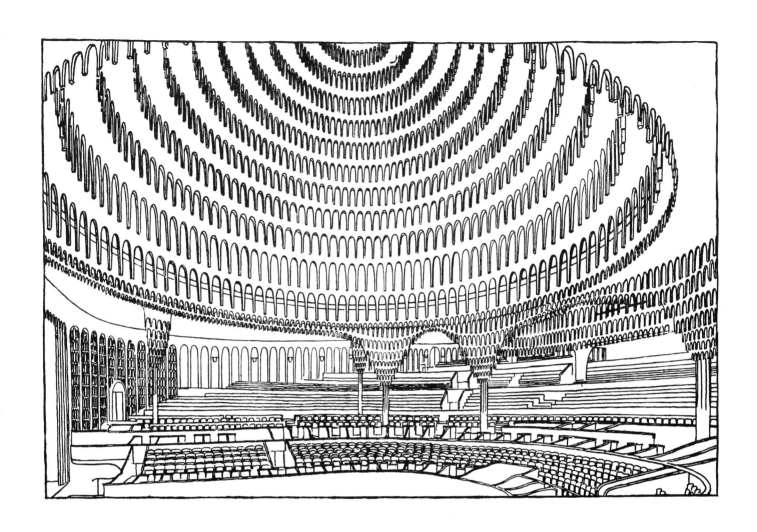

27 Hans Poelzig (1918/19)

28 Hans Poelzig 1925

46

29 Peter Behrens (1920–24)

30 Ludwig Mies van der Rohe 1919

31 Hugo Häring 1922

32 Dominikus Böhm 1922

33 Gottfried Böhm 1965

34 Frank Lloyd Wright 1959

35 Bruce Goff 1949

36 Jørn Utzon 1958

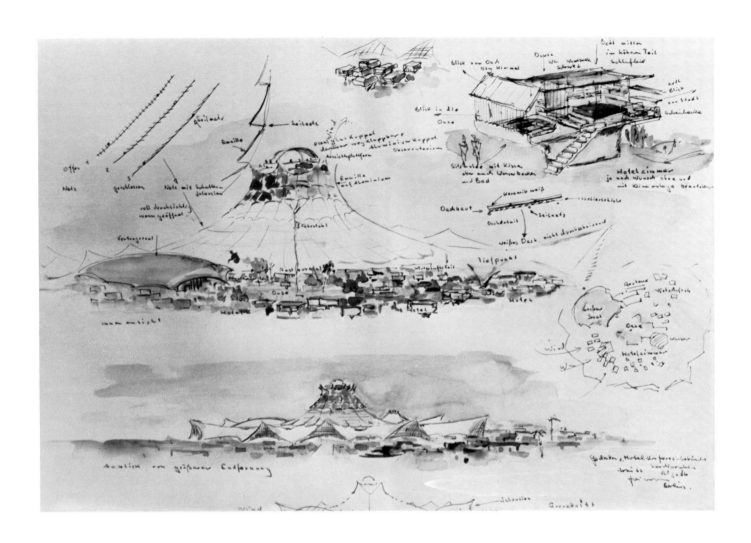

37 Frei Otto 1966

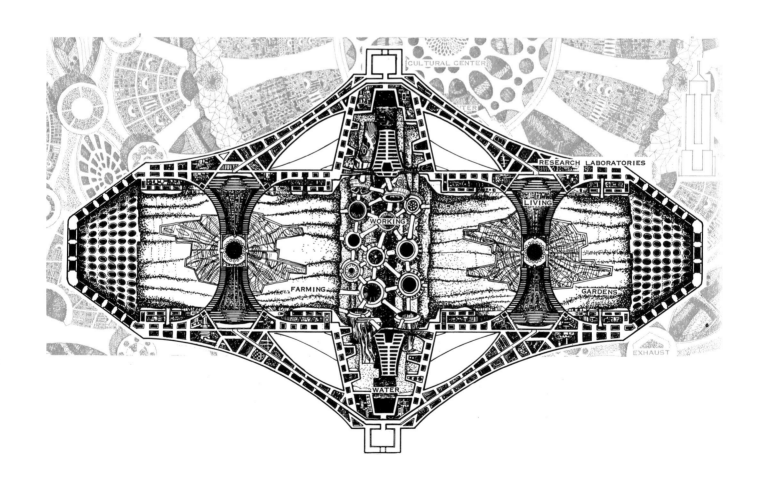

Labels visible within the illustration: CULTURAL CENTER, RESEARCH LABORATORIES, LIVING, WORKING, FARMING, GARDENS, WATER, EXHAUST

38 Paolo Soleri 1967

39 Peter Cook, Christine Hawley 1979

See, therein lies the greatness of our age, that it is incapable of producing a new ornament. We have outgrown ornament; we have fought our way through to freedom from ornament. See, the time is nigh, fulfillment awaits us. Soon the streets of the city will glisten like white walls. Like Zion, the holy city, the capital of heaven. Then fulfillment will be come.

Adolf Loos, 1908[13]

In modern times, the process of the consistent stylistic evolution of architecture has come to a stop. "Architecture is breaking free from tradition. It must perforce begin again from the beginning."
The calculation of the strength of materials, the use of reinforced concrete, rule out "architecture" in the classical and traditional sense. Modern building materials and our scientific ideas absolutely do not lend themselves to the disciplines of historical styles. ...
The tremendous antithesis between the modern and the ancient world is the outcome of all those things that exist now and did not exist then. Elements have entered into our life of whose very possibility the ancients did not even dream. Material possibilities and attitudes of mind have come into being that have had a thousand repercussions, first and foremost of which is the creation of a new ideal of beauty, still obscure and embryonic, but whose fascination is already being felt even by the masses. We have lost the sense of the monumental, of the heavy, of the static; we have enriched our sensibility by a "taste for the light, the practical, the ephemeral and the swift." We feel that we are no longer the men of the cathedrals, the palaces, the assembly halls; but of big hotels, railway stations, immense roads, colossal ports, covered markets, brilliantly lit galleries, freeways, demolition and rebuilding schemes.

Antonio Sant'Elia, 1914[14]

Architecture is the masterly, correct and magnificent play of masses brought together in light. Our eyes are made to see forms in light; light and shade reveal these forms; cubes, cones, spheres, cylinders or pyramids are the great primary forms which light reveals to advantage; the image of these is distinct and tangible within us and without ambiguity. It is for that reason that these are *beautiful forms, the most beautiful forms*. Everybody is agreed as to that, the child, the savage and the metaphysician. It is of the very nature or the plastic arts. ...
Architecture is governed by standards. Standards are a matter of logic, analysis and precise study. Standards are based on a problem which has been well stated. Architecture means plastic invention, intellectual speculation, higher mathematics. Architecture is a very noble art.
Standardization is imposed by the law of selection and is an economic and social necessity. Harmony is a state of agreement with the norms of our universe. Beauty governs all; she is of purely human creation; she is the overplus necessary only to men of the highest type.

Le Corbusier, 1923[15]

The new and true architecture must result from a close connection with logic, rationalism. The rules must be determined by a strict constructivism. The new architectural forms must derive their aesthetic value solely from the character of the need. Only then, through selection, will style be born. Hence we do not intend to create a style (similar attempts to create something out of nothing have brought results like the "liberty"); style will come through a process of selection in the constant use of rationality, through the perfect unity between the structure of the building and its purpose. What is bound to be achieved is the ennoblement of constructivism through the undefinable and abstract perfection of pure rhythm. Of itself simple constructivism would not be beautiful.

Gruppo 7 (Ubaldo Castagnoli, Luigi Figini, Guido Frette, Sebastiano Larco, Gino Pollini, Carlo Enrico Rava, Giuseppe Terragni), 1926/27[16]

Every decision leads to a special kind of order.
Therefore we must make clear what principles of order are possible and clarify them.
Let us recognize that the mechanistic principle of order overemphasizes the materialistic and functionalistic factors in life, since it fails to satisfy our feeling that means must be subsidiary to ends and our desire for dignity and value.
The idealistic principle of order, however, with its over-emphasis on the ideal and the formal, satisfies neither our interest in simple reality nor our practical sense.
So we shall emphasize the organic principle of order as a means of achieving the successful relationship of the parts to each other and to the whole.
And here we shall take our stand.
The long path from material through function to creative work has only a single goal: to create order out of the desperate confusion of our time.
We must have order, allocating to each thing its proper place and giving to each thing its due according to its nature.
We would do this so perfectly that the world of our creations will blossom from within.
We want no more; we can do no more.

Ludwig Mies van der Rohe, 1938[17]

The making of form can, for instance, be considered as a problem of logical consistency; as a consequence of the logical structure inherent in any formal relationship. The making of form in this sense is more than the satisfaction of functional requirements and more than the creation of aesthetically pleasing objects, but rather the exposition of a set of formal relationships. ...
The thesis presented ... is as follows: one way of producing an environment which can accept or give a more precise and richer meaning than at present, is to understand the nature of the structure of form itself, as opposed to the relationship of form to function or of form to meaning.

Peter Eisenman, 1969[18]

40+41 Tony Garnier (1901–04)

42 Tony Garnier (1901–04)

43 Tony Garnier (1901–04)

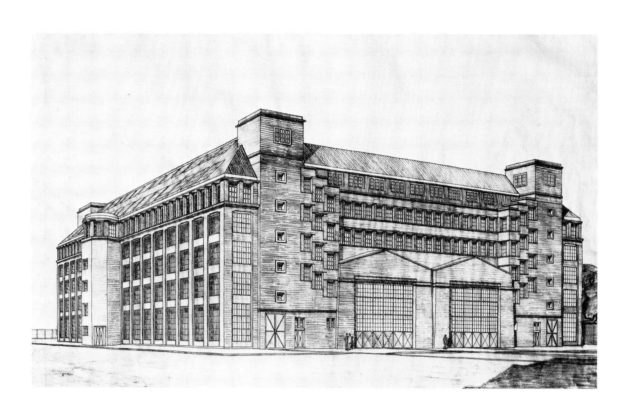

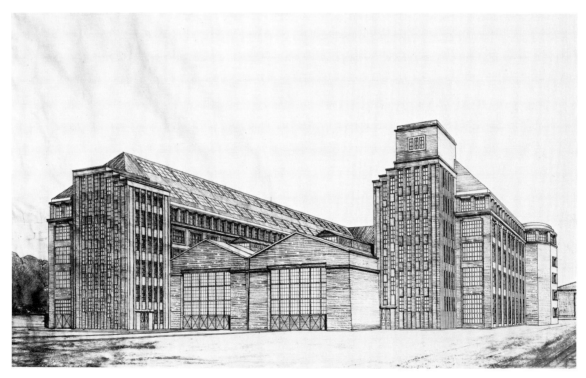

44+45 Peter Behrens 1909

46 Peter Behrens 1911/12

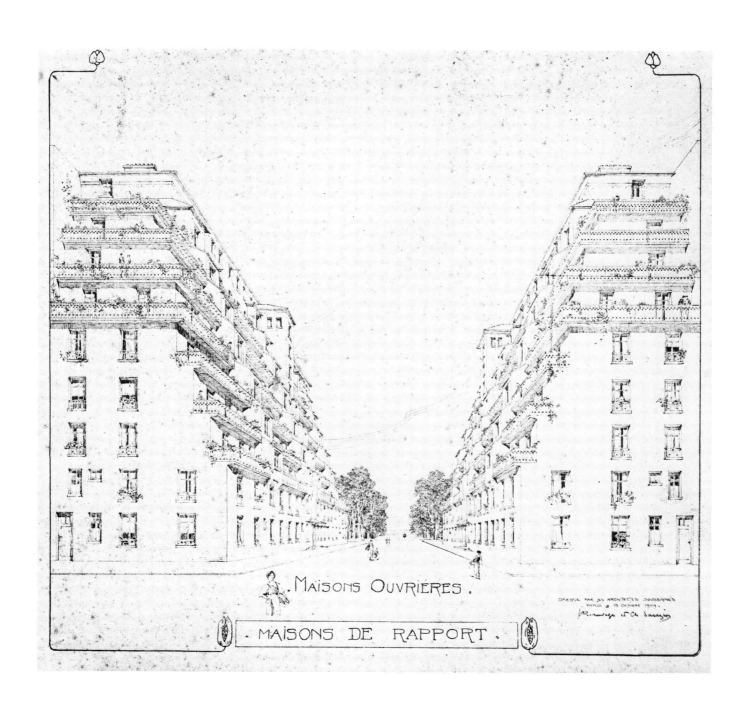

47 Henri Sauvage, Charles Sarazin 1909

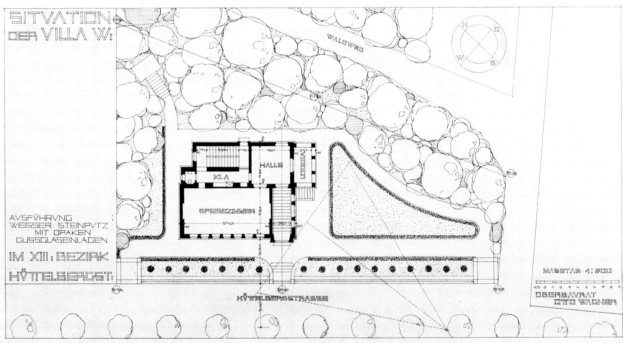

48 Otto Wagner 1905

49 Antonio Sant'Elia 1914

50 Antonio Sant'Elia 1914

51 Antonio Sant'Elia 1913

52 Antonio Sant'Elia 1913/14

53 Mario Chiattone 1914

54 El Lissitzky, Mart Stam 1924

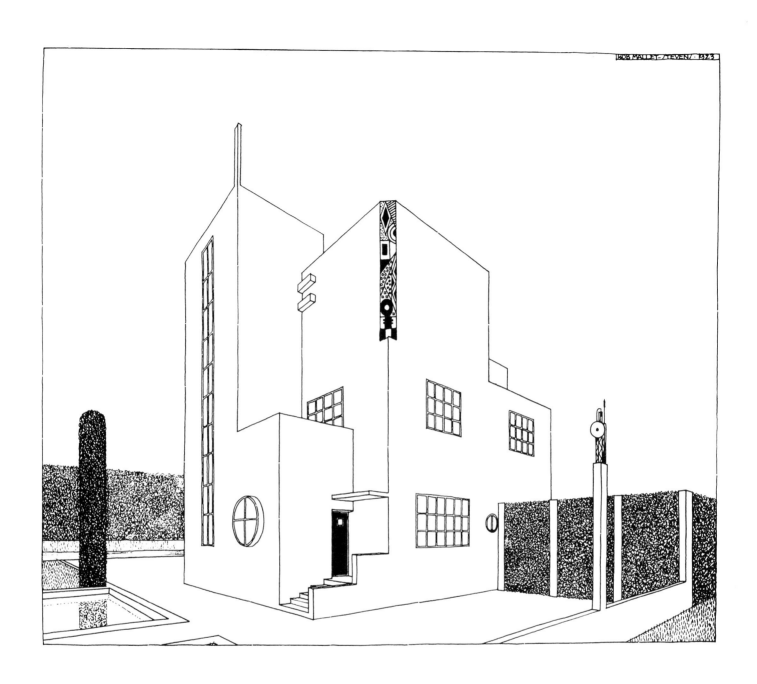

55 Rob Mallet-Stevens 1923

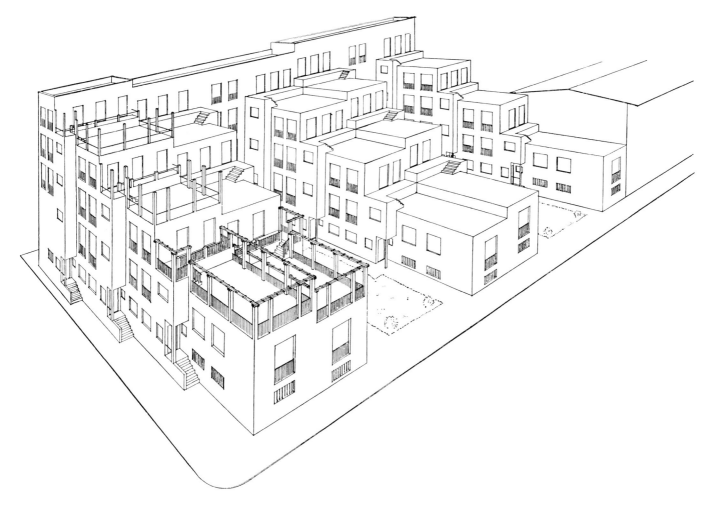

56 Adolf Loos 1923

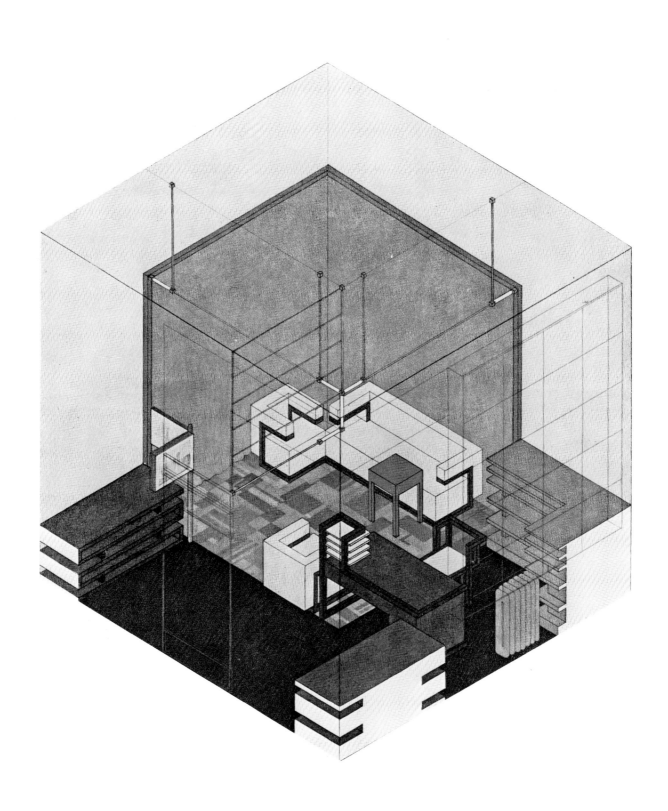

57 Walter Gropius (1923)

74

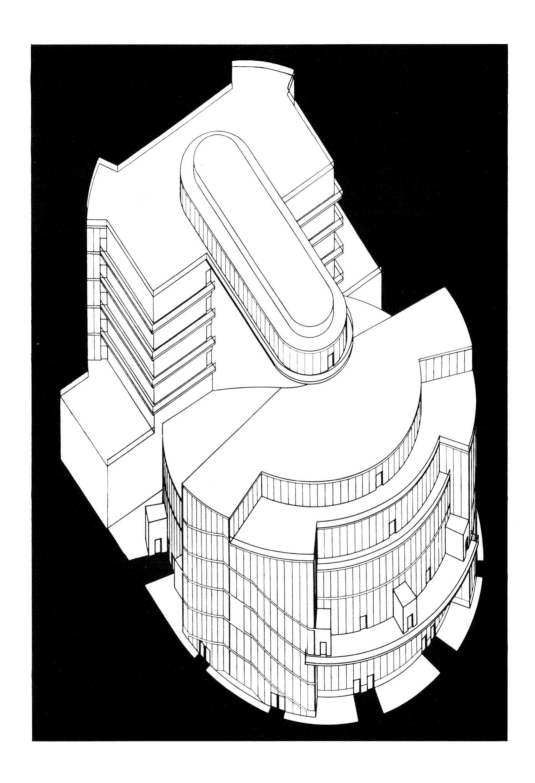

58 Walter Gropius 1927

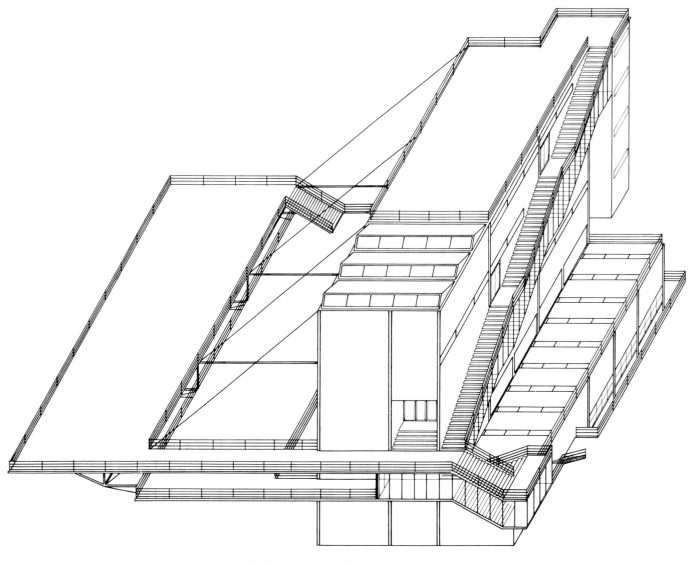

59 Hannes Meyer, Hans Wittwer 1926

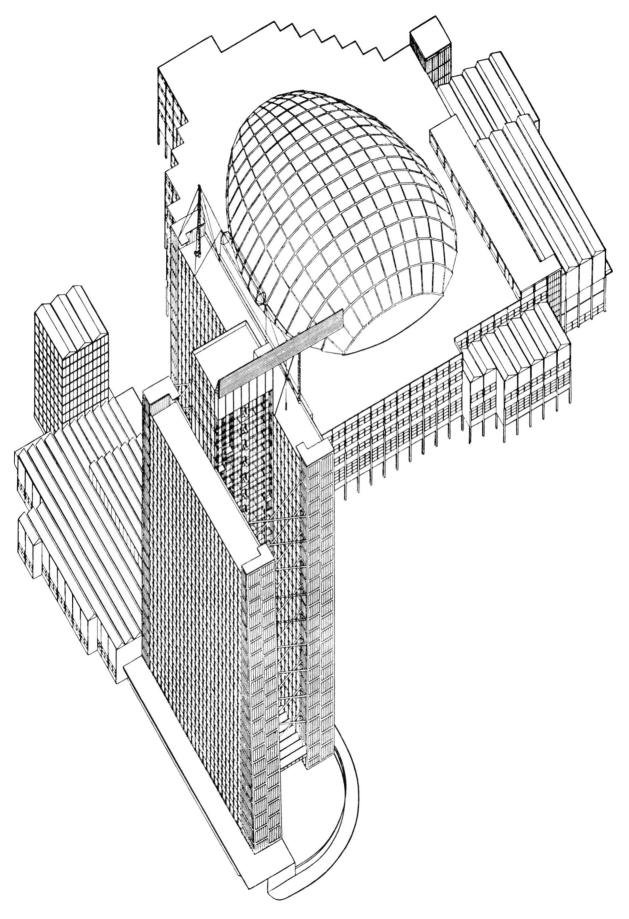

60 Hannes Meyer, Hans Wittwer 1927

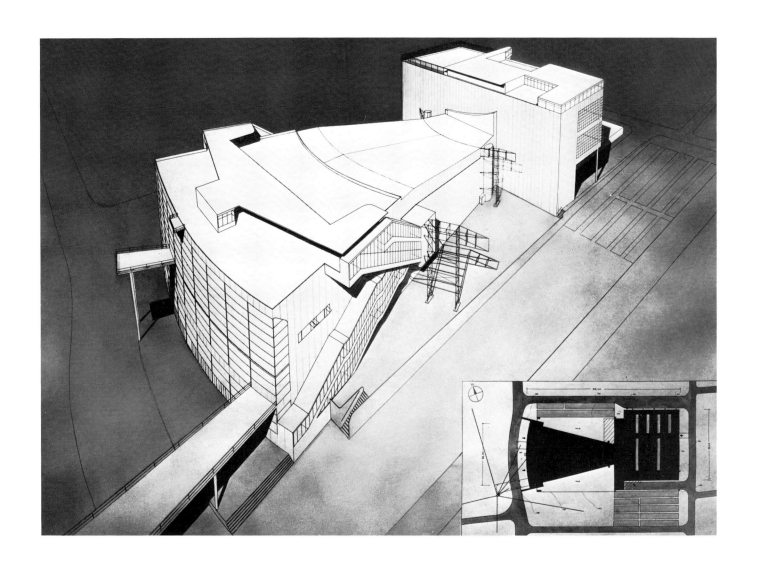

61 Marcel Breuer 1930

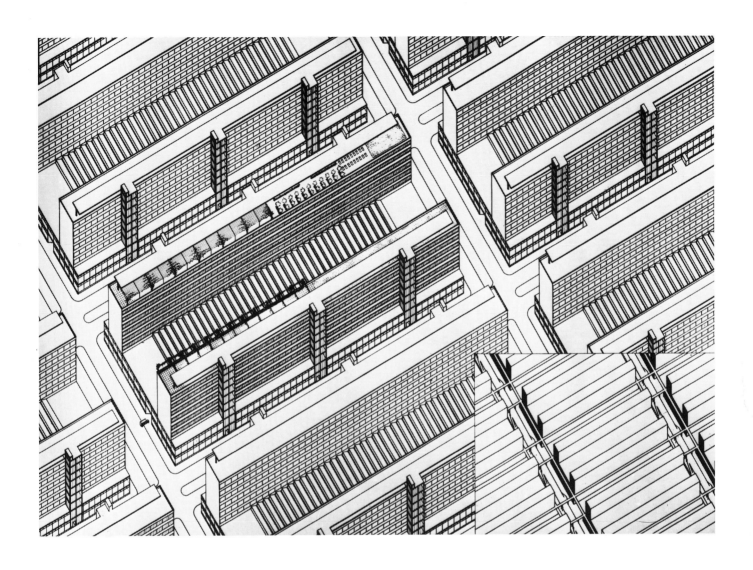

62 Ludwig Hilberseimer 1926

63 Ludwig Mies van der Rohe 1922

64 Ludwig Mies van der Rohe 1933

65 Ludwig Mies van der Rohe 1935

66 Ludwig Mies van der Rohe 1939

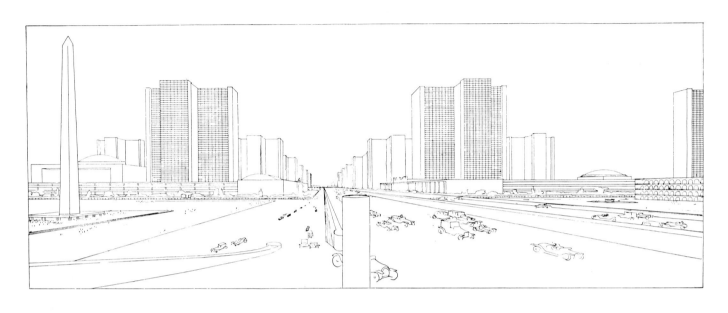

67 Le Corbusier 1922

68 Le Corbusier 1927

69 Le Corbusier 1928

70 Le Corbusier 1928

71 Le Corbusier 1929

72 Le Corbusier 1942

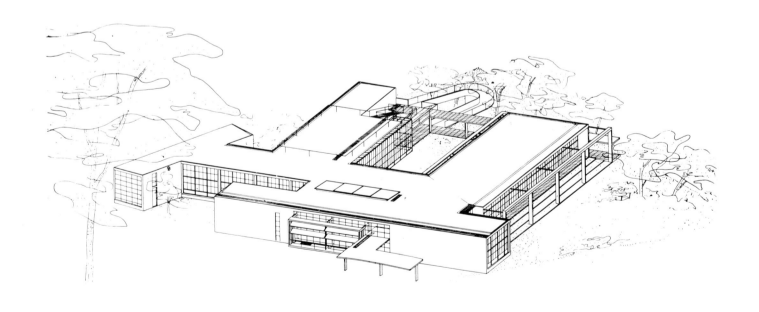

73 Giuseppe Terragni 1936/37

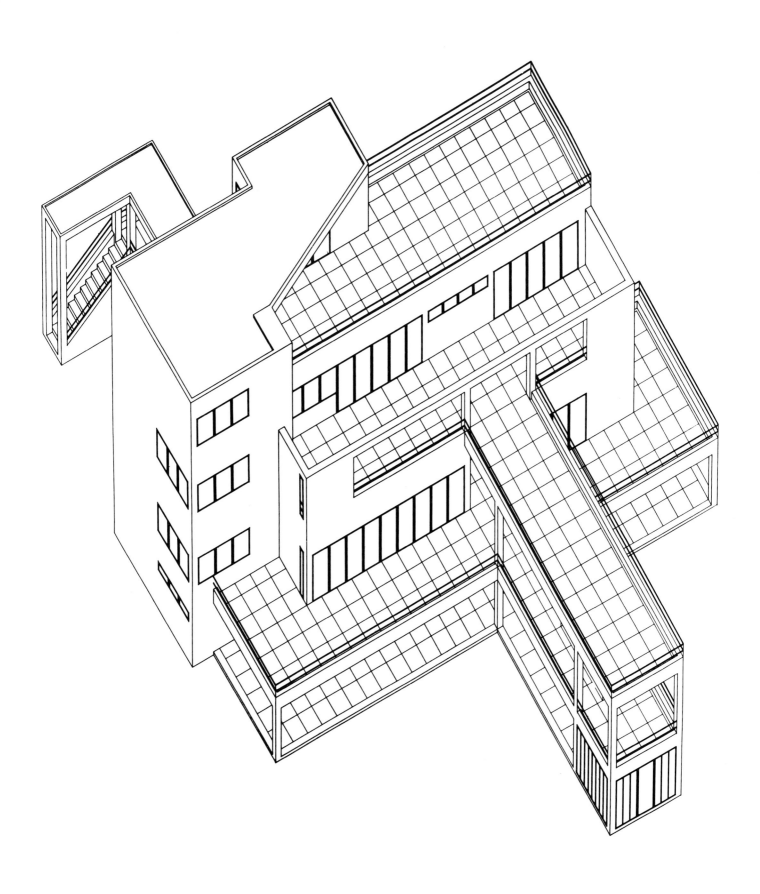

74 Alberto Sartoris 1937

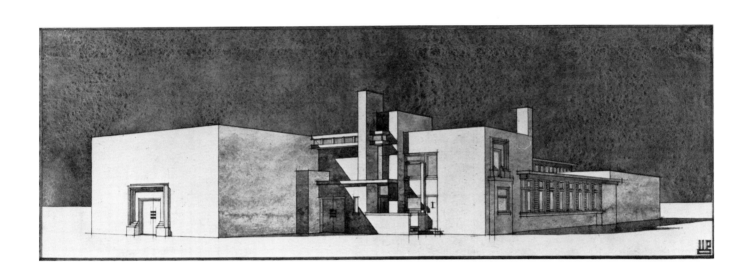

75 Jacobus Johannes Pieter Oud 1919

76 Jacobus Johannes Pieter Oud 1931

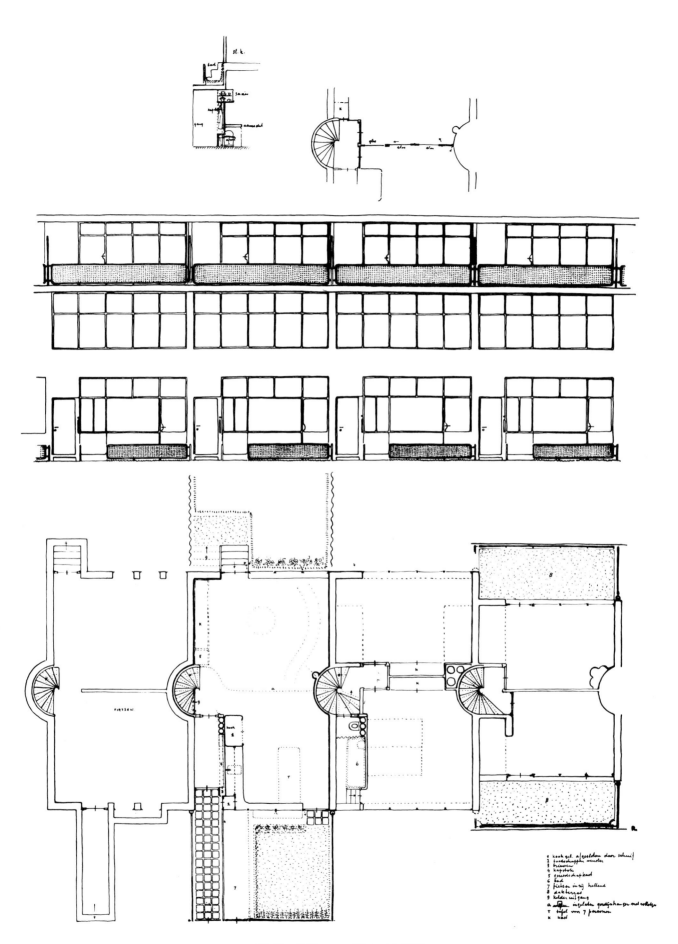

77 Gerrit Thomas Rietveld 1931

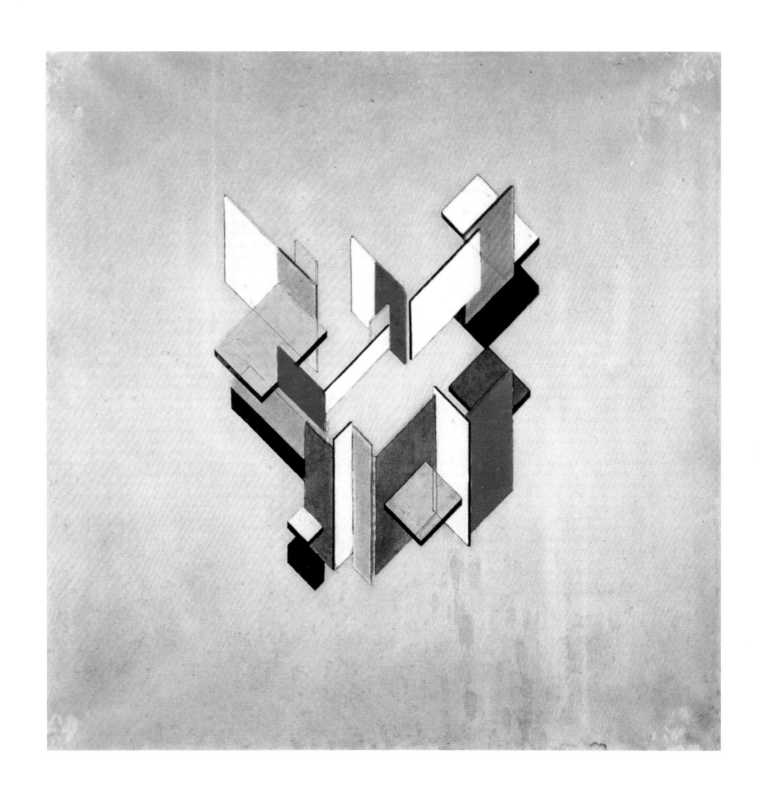

78 Theo van Doesburg 1923

79 Willem Marinus Dudok 1924

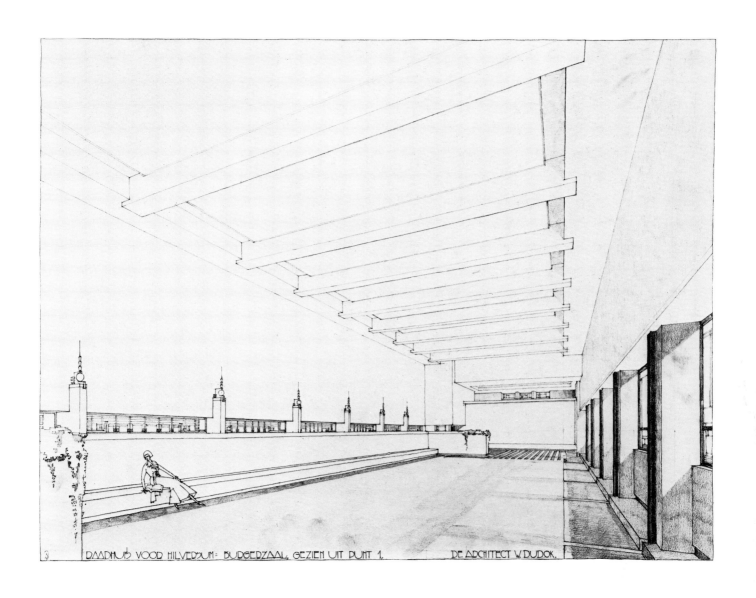

RAADHUIS VOOR HILVERSUM: BURGERZAAL, GEZIEN UIT PUNT 1,   DE ARCHITECT W. DUDOK.

80 Willem Marinus Dudok 1924

THE PLAY MART R.M. SCHINDLER

81 Rudolf Schindler 1921

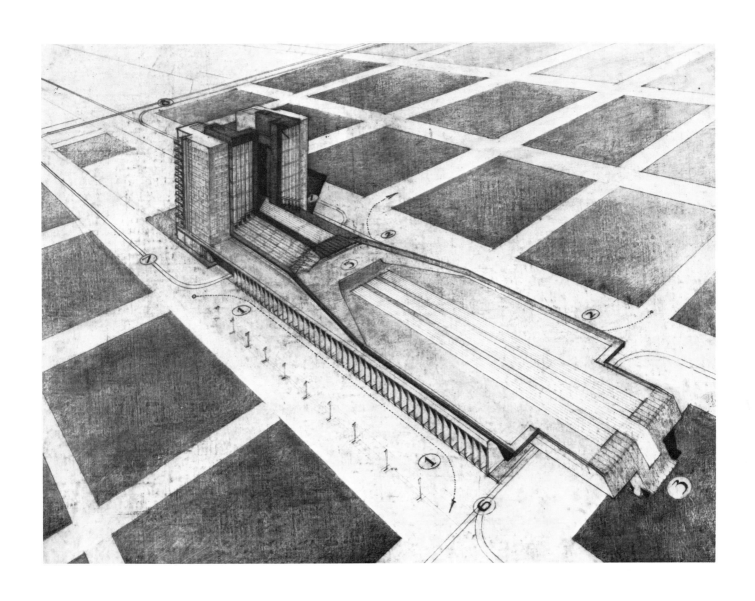

82 Richard Neutra (1927)

99

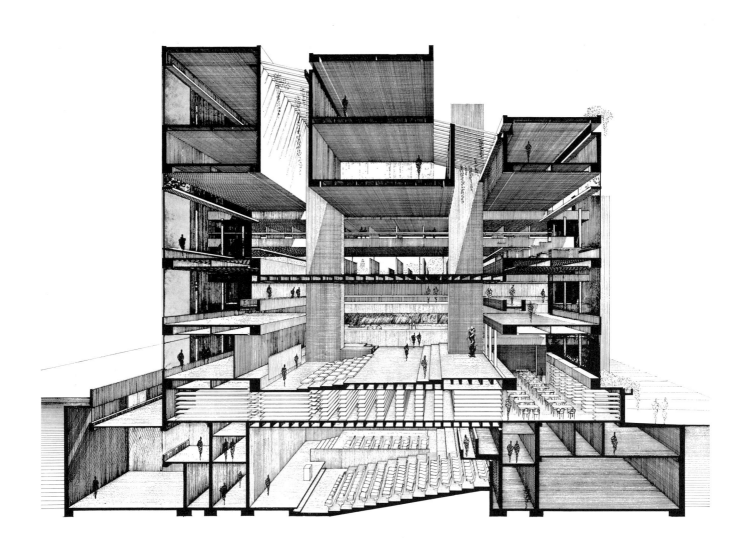

83 Paul Rudolph 1958

84 Paul Rudolph 1965

85 Cesar Pelli & Associates 1980

102

86 Cesar Pelli & Associates 1977

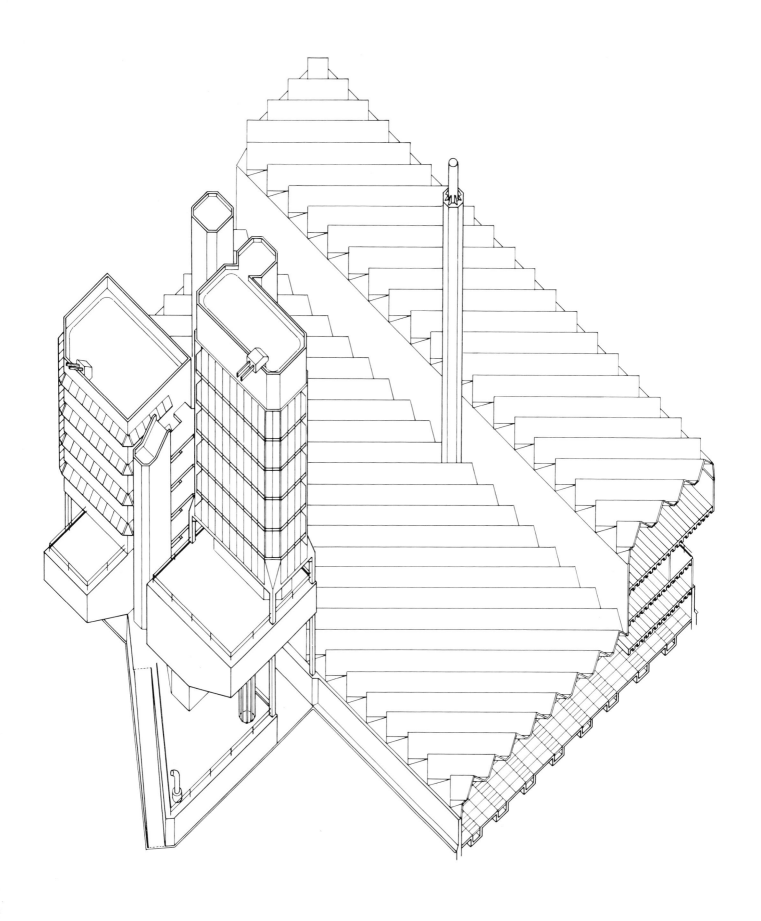

87 James Stirling, James Gowan 1959

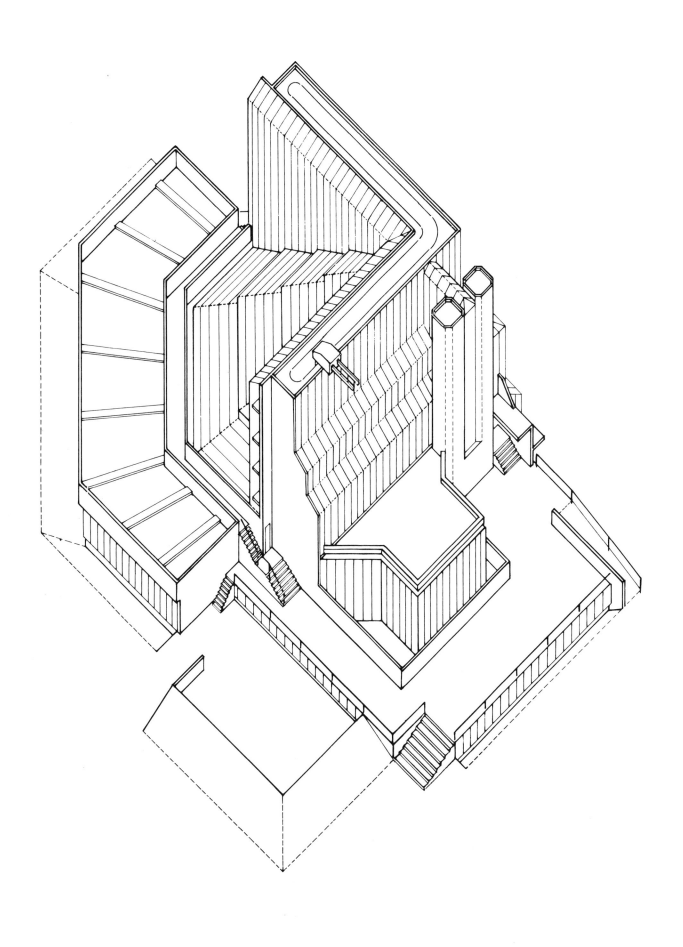

88 James Stirling 1964

105

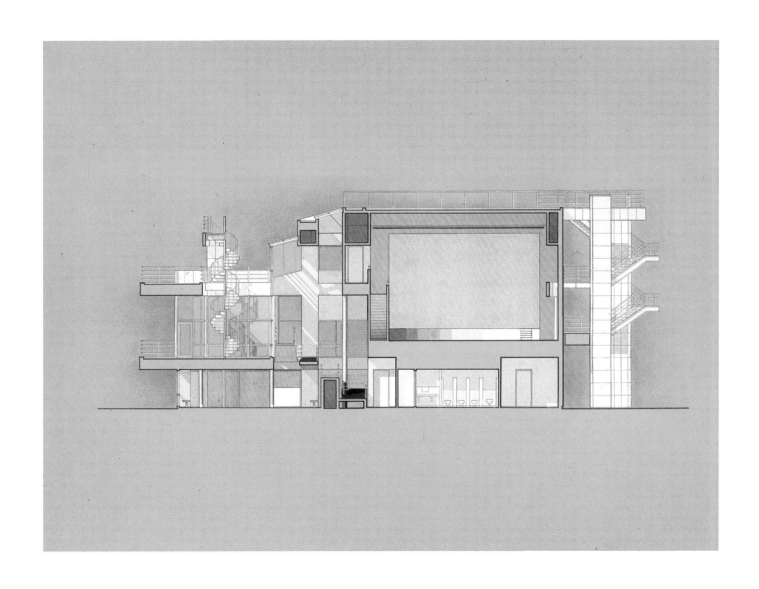

89 Richard Meier & Partners 1979

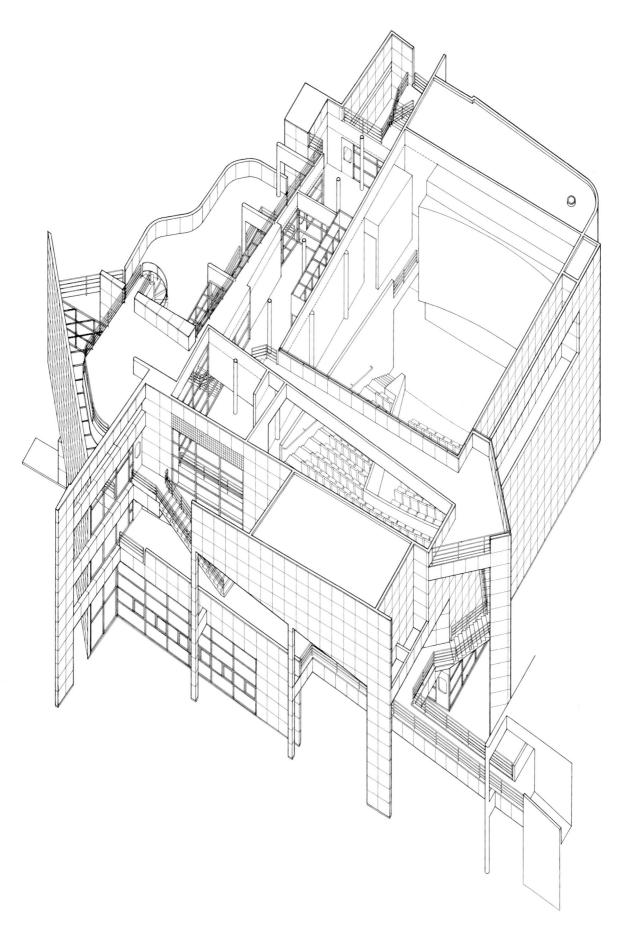

90 Richard Meier & Partners 1976

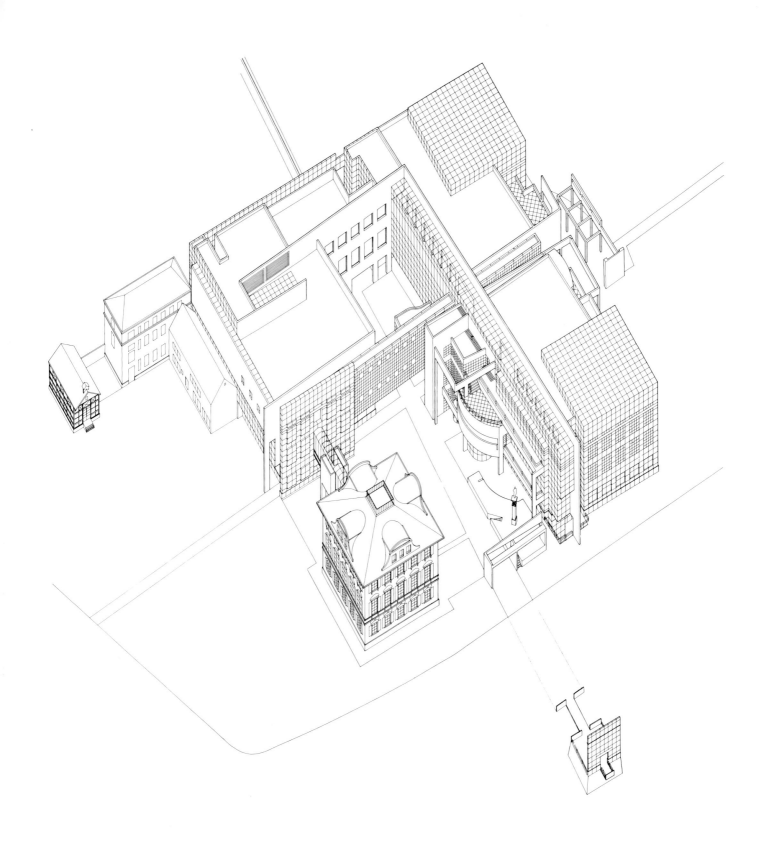

91 Richard Meier & Partners 1979

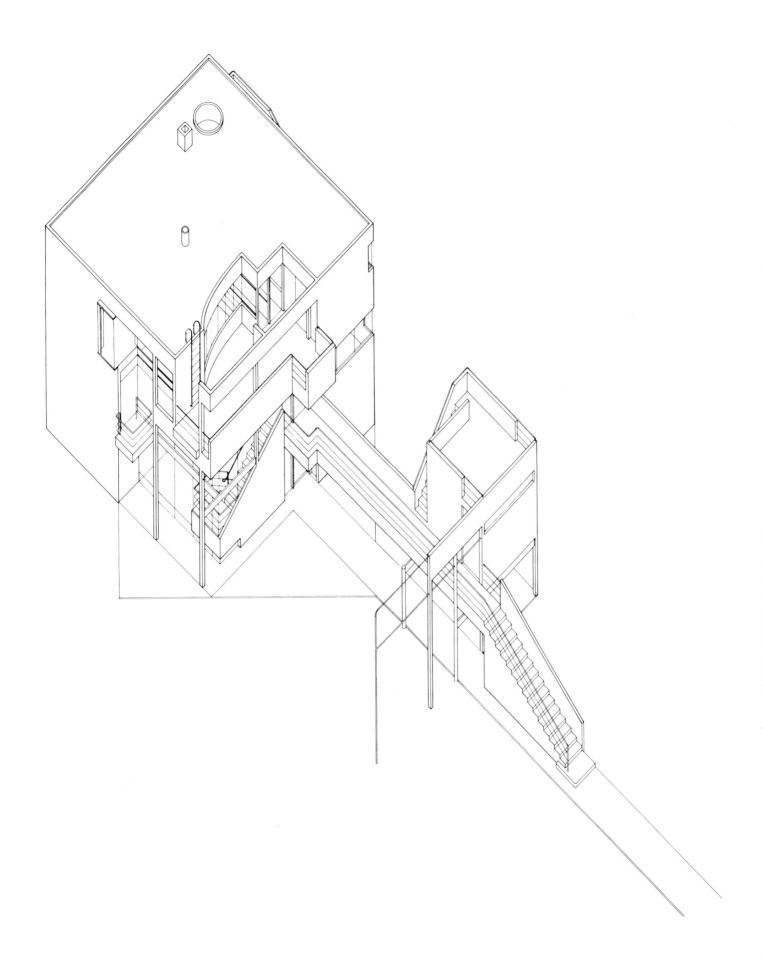

92 Michael Graves 1969

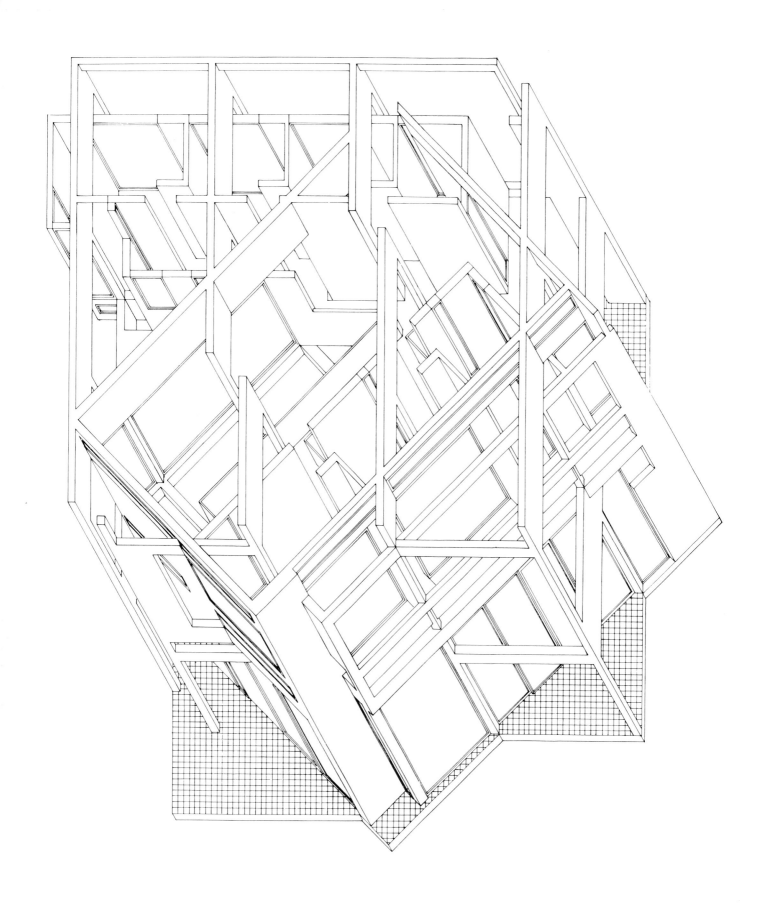

93 Peter Eisenman (1969/70)

110

94 Peter Eisenman 1978

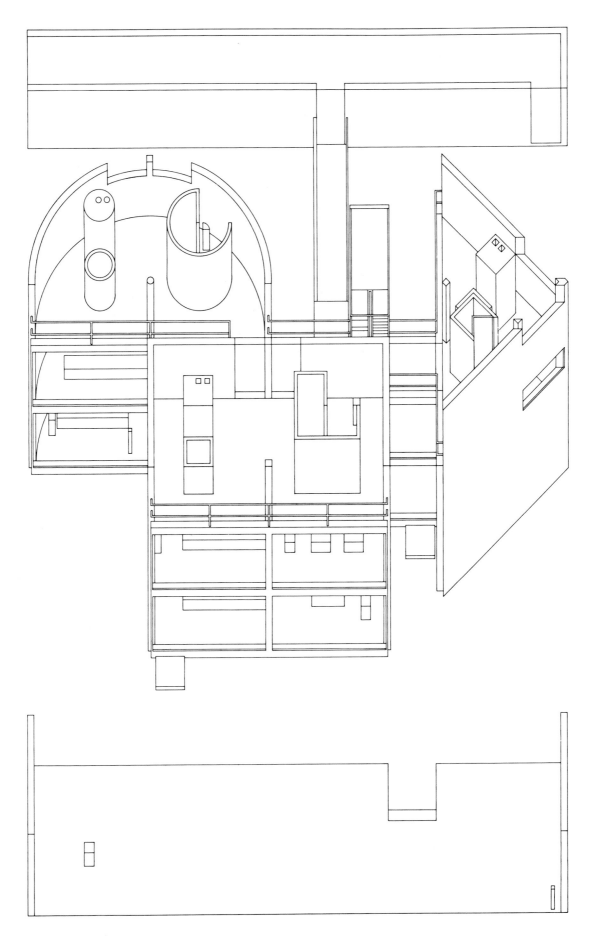

95 John Hejduk 1966

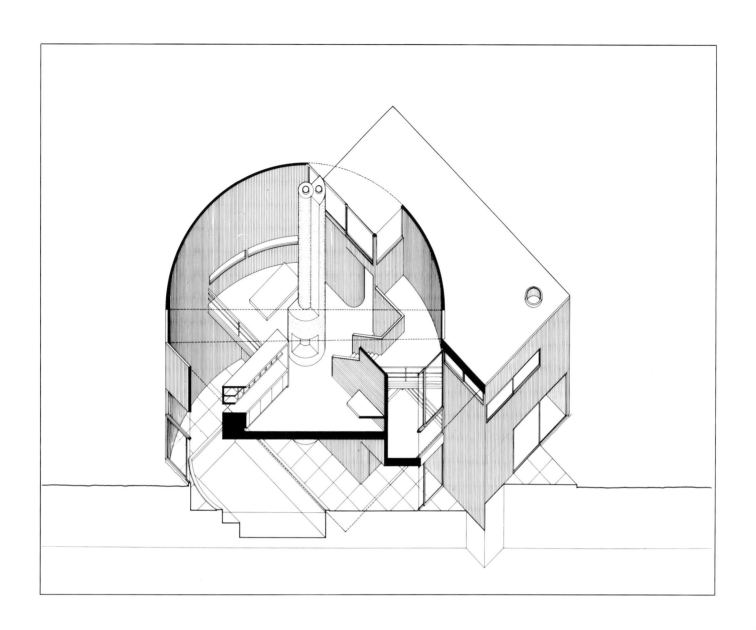

96 Charles Gwathmey 1969

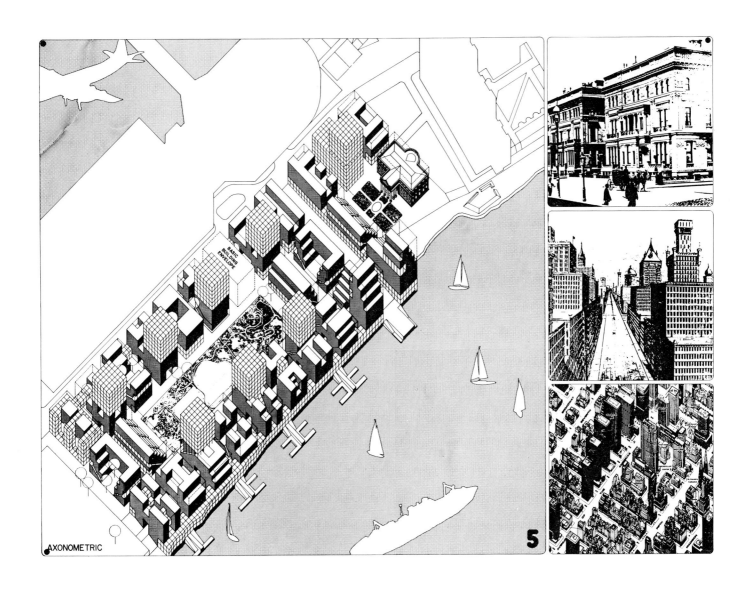

AXONOMETRIC

BASIC BUILDING ENVELOPE

5

97 Oswald Mathias Ungers 1975

98 Elia Zenghelis, Zoe Zenghelis/OMA 1975

The problem of Futurist architecture is not a problem of linear rearrangement. It is not a question of finding new profiles, new door and window frames, substitutes for columns, pilasters, consoles, caryatids, gargoyles. It is not a question of leaving the façade bare brick, painting it or facing it with stone; nor of establishing formal differences between new and old buildings. It is a question of creating the Futurist house according to a sound plan, of building it with the aid of every scientific and technical resource, of fulfilling to the limit every demand of our way of life and our spirit, of rejecting everything grotesque, cumbrous, and alien to us (tradition, style, aesthetic, proportion), establishing new forms, new lines, a new harmony of profiles and volumes, an architecture whose raison d'être lies solely in the special conditions of modern life, whose aesthetic values are in perfect harmony with our sensibility. This architecture cannot be subject to any law of historical continuity. It must be as new as our frame of mind is new. ...

We must invent and rebuild the Futurist city: it must be like an immense, tumultuous, lively, noble work site, dynamic in all its parts; and the Futurist house must be like an enormous machine. The lifts must not hide like lonely worms in the stair wells; the stairs, become useless, must be done away with and the lifts must climb like serpents of iron and glass up the housefronts. The house of concrete, glass, and iron, without painting and without sculpture, enriched solely by the innate beauty of its lines and projections, extremely "ugly" in its mechanical simplicity, high and wide as prescribed by local government regulations, must rise on the edge of a tumultuous abyss. ...

"The decorative must be abolished." The problem of Futurist architecture must be solved not by plagiarizing China, Persia, or Japan with the aid of photographs, not by foolishly adhering to the rules of Vitruvius, but by strokes of genius and armed with scientific and technical experience. Everything must be revolutionary.

Antonio Sant'Elia, 1914[19]

Technology is rooted in the past.
It dominates the present and tends into the future.
It is a real historical movement –
one of the great movements which shape and represent their epoch.
It can be compared only with the Classic discovery of man as a person,
the Roman will to power,
and the religious movement of the Middle Ages.
Technology is far more than a method,
it is a world in itself.

Ludwig Mies van der Rohe, 1950[20]

Science and technology make possible the establishment of tasks whose solution demands precise study before end results can be formulated.
The machine is the tool of our age. It is the cause of those effects through which the social order manifests itself.
New materials, methods, processes, knowledge in the fields of statics and dynamics, planning techniques and sociological conditions must be accepted.

The building must evolve indirectly, obeying the conditions of industrialization, through the multiplication of cells and elements.
Modular systems of co-ordination, scientific experimental methods, the laws of automation, and precision influence creative thought.
Very complex static and mechanical problems demand the closest possible co-operation with industry and specialists in ideal teams composed of masters.
Human and aesthetic ideas will receive new impulses through the uncompromising application of contemporary knowledge and ability.

Konrad Wachsmann, 1957[21]

We are not trying to make houses like cars, cities like oil refineries, even if we seem to be ... this analogous imagery ... will eventually be digested into a creative system ... Yet it has become necessary to extend ourselves into such disciplines in order to discover an appropriate language to the present-day situation.

Warren Chalk, 1971[22]

Provisional architecture is aggressive. It breaks with old ways of seeing. It is a school for astonishment and it has sharp accentuations; tailor-made for any situation, these can provide uncompromising solutions to problems. They are free of the constraints of local politics and utilitarian considerations because they are not mortgaged to the need to exist for the next hundred years. Provisional structures make no claim to perfection. What matters is the directness of the solutions, not the polish on detail. Provisional architecture will not build a cathedral, nor will it create candle shops, it merely *simulates possible changes*. And it can be cleared away.

Laurids Ortner, 1976[23]

But we do not feel like building Biedermeier. Not now and not at any time. We are sick of seeing Palladio and all the other masks from history. Because we do not want to exclude from architecture anything that causes unease.
We want an architecture which has more. An architecture which bleeds, which exhausts, which turns and as far as I am concerned breaks. An architecture which shines, which stings, which tears and splits if stretched. Architecture must be engulfing, fiery, smooth, hard, with sharp corners. It must be brutal, round, tender, coloured, obscene, lurid, dreaming, enticing, distancing, wet, dry and heartbeating. It must be living or dead. If it is cold, then it must be as cold as an ice block. If it is hot, then it must be as hot as a sheet of fire.
Architecture must burn.

Coop Himmelblau, 1980[24]

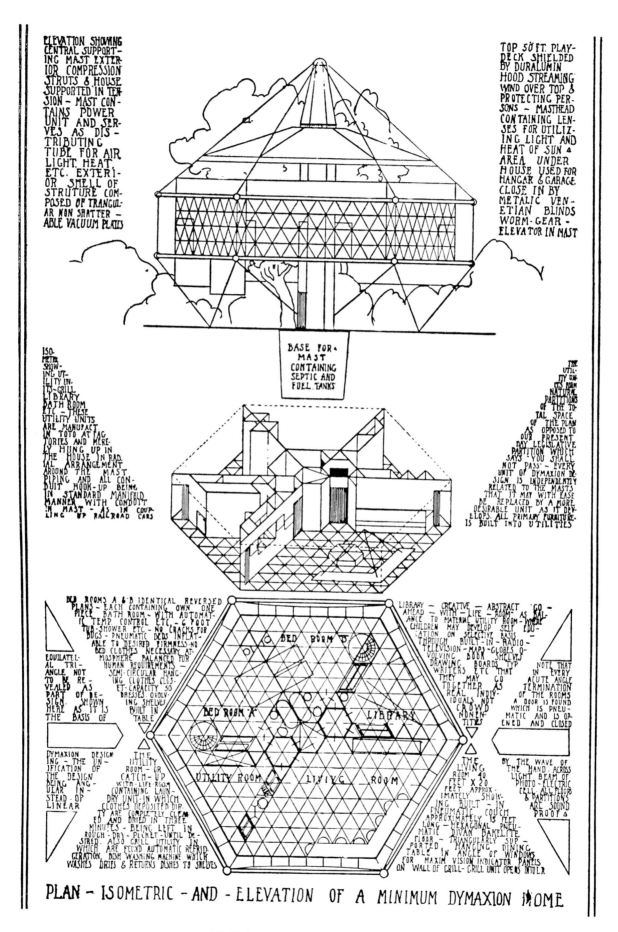

PLAN · ISOMETRIC · AND · ELEVATION · OF · A · MINIMUM · DYMAXION · HOME

99 Richard Buckminster Fuller 1927

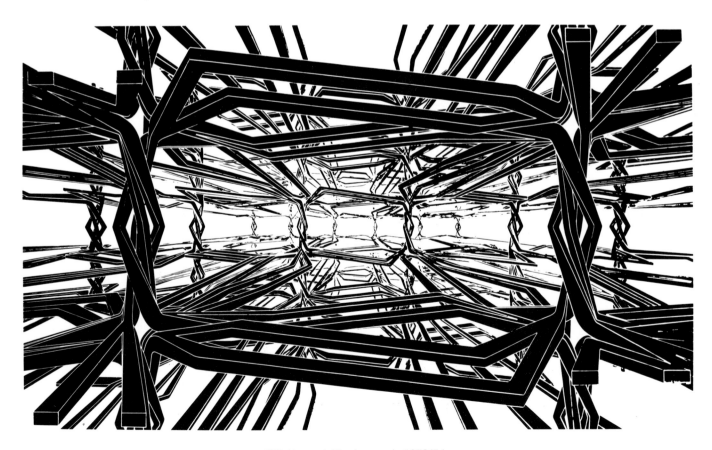

100 Konrad Wachsmann 1953/54

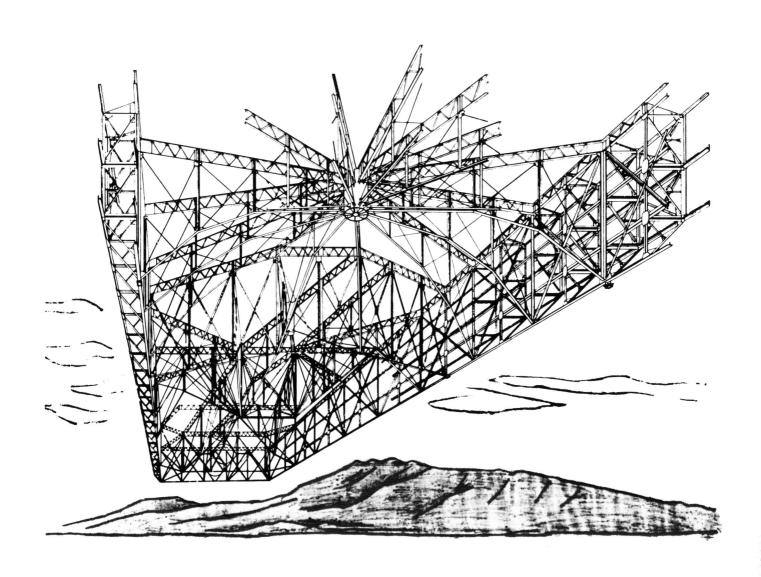

101 Kiyonori Kikutake 1969

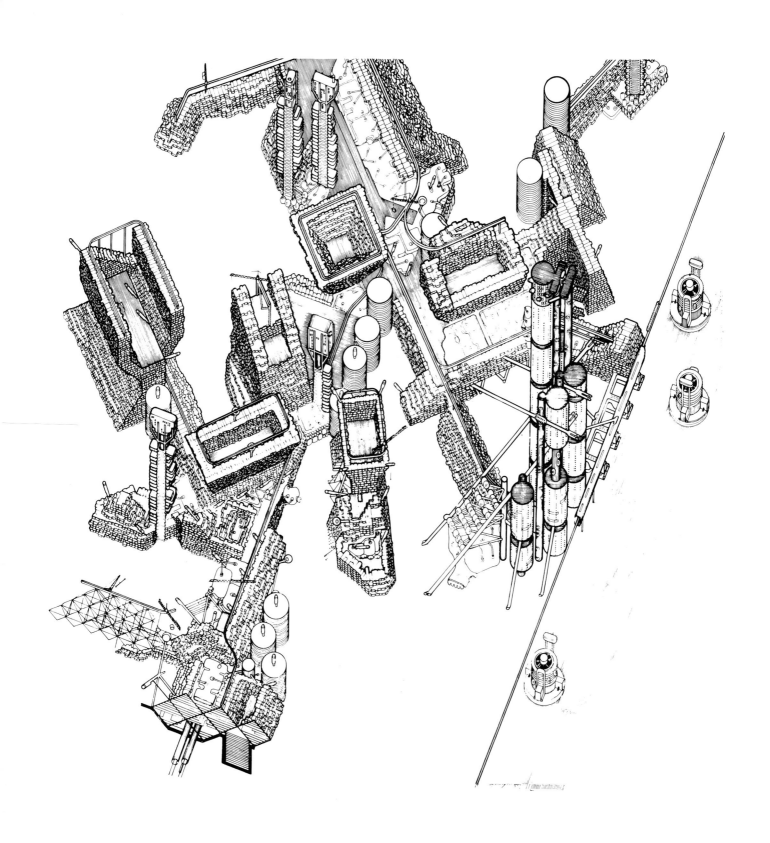

102 Peter Cook 1964

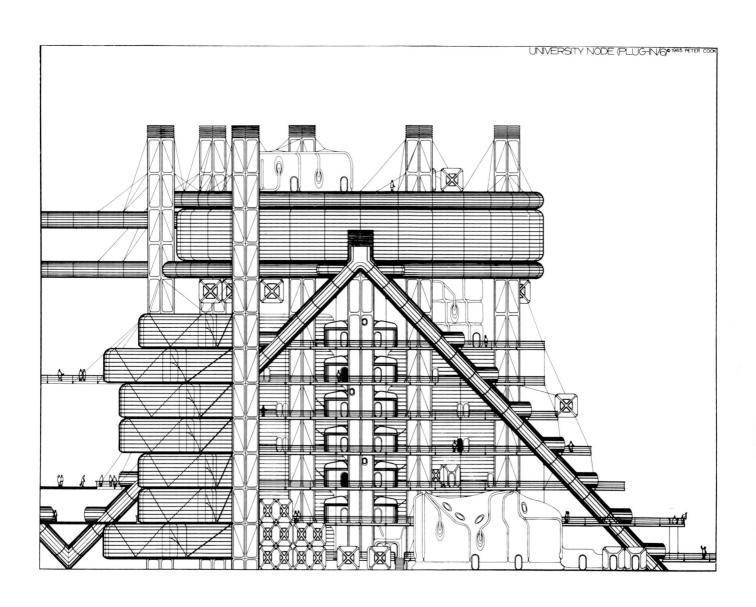

103 Peter Cook 1965

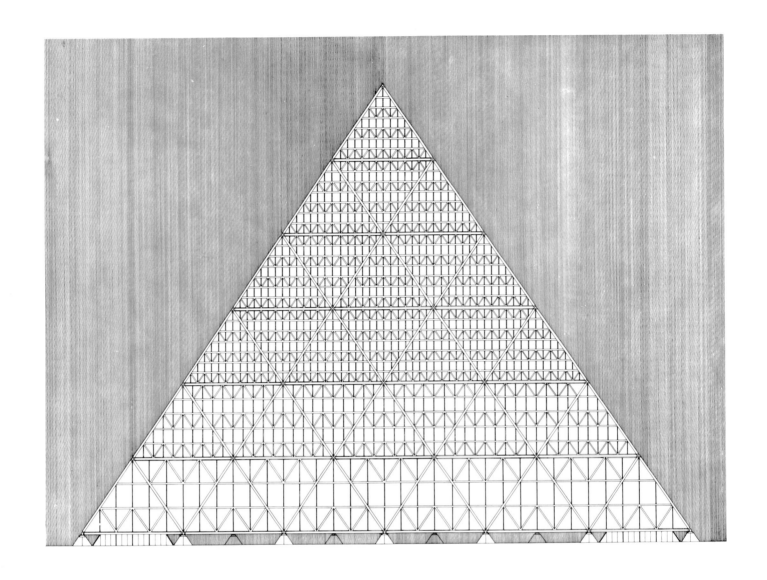

104 Stanley Tigerman 1968

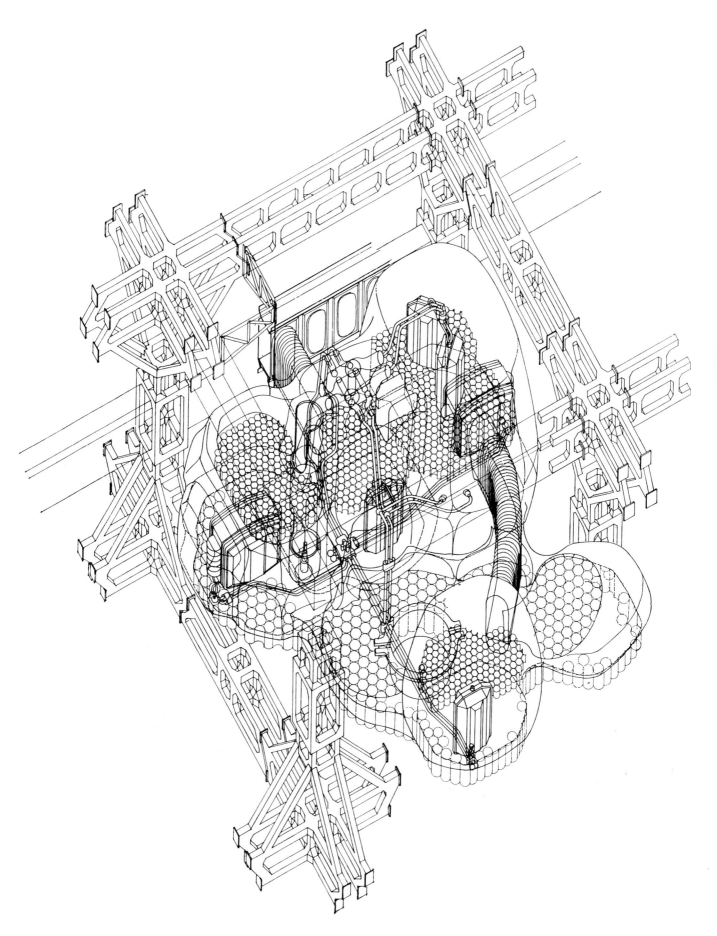

105 Günther Domenig und Eilfried Huth (1966–69)

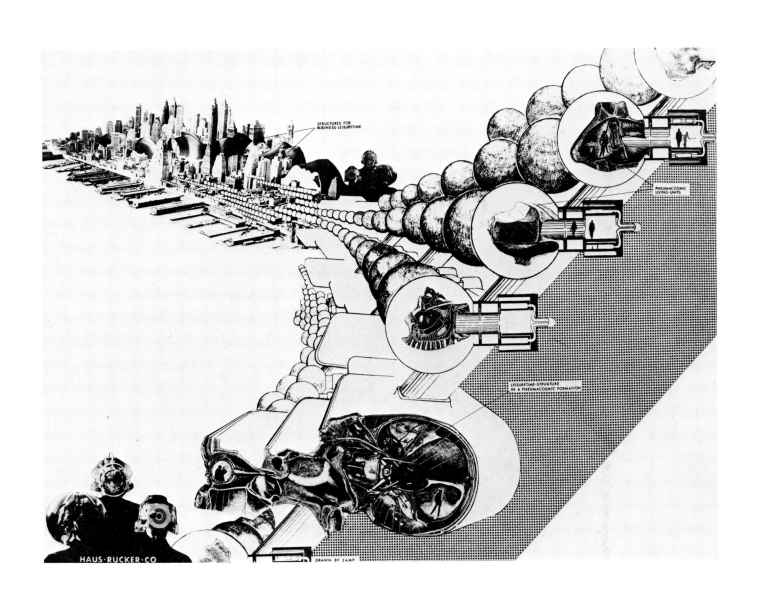

106 Haus-Rucker-Co 1967/68

107 Haus-Rucker-Co 1977

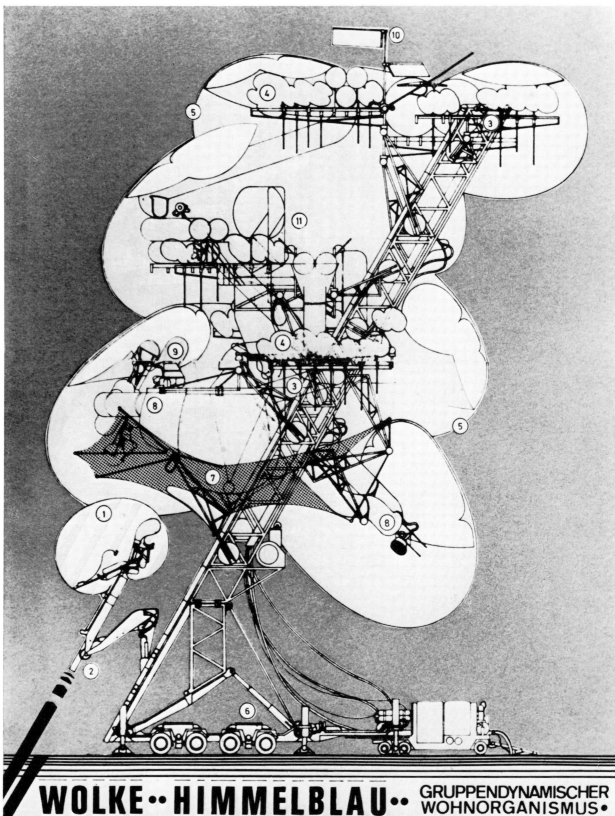

WOLKE ·· HIMMELBLAU ·· GRUPPENDYNAMISCHER WOHNORGANISMUS ·

① PROMOTER ② BLITZ (hydraul. Arm) ③ METAMORPHE TRAG + VERSORGUNGSSTRUKTUR ④ PN. EUMOLANDSCHAFT ⑤ SCHWEBENDE KLIMAHAUT ⑥ FAHRGESTELL ⑦ SPRUNGNETZ ⑧ SCHWIM M + TAUCHGARTEN ⑨ NAHRUNGS - AUTOMATEN ⑩ SONNENDECK ⑪ SANITÄRBLOCK

108 Coop Himmelblau 1968

109 Coop Himmelblau (1968–72)

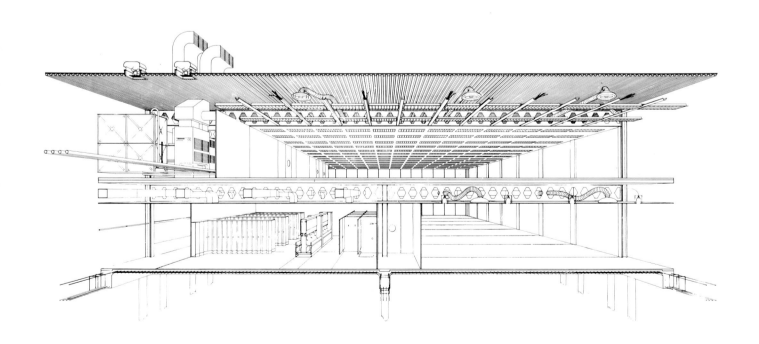

110 Foster Associates 1969

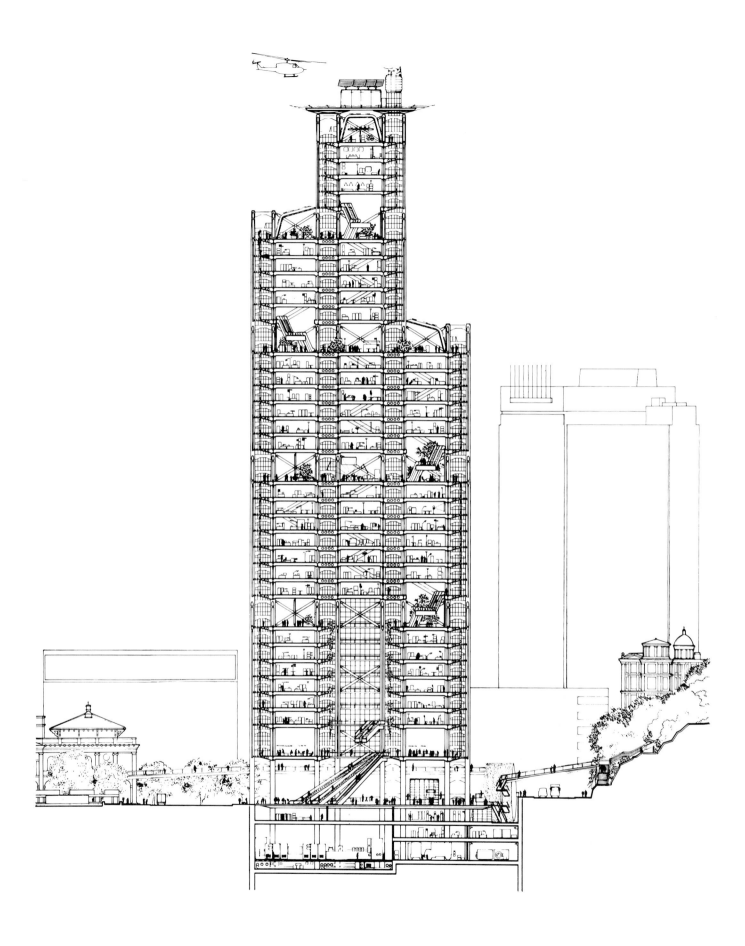

111 Foster Associates 1981

129

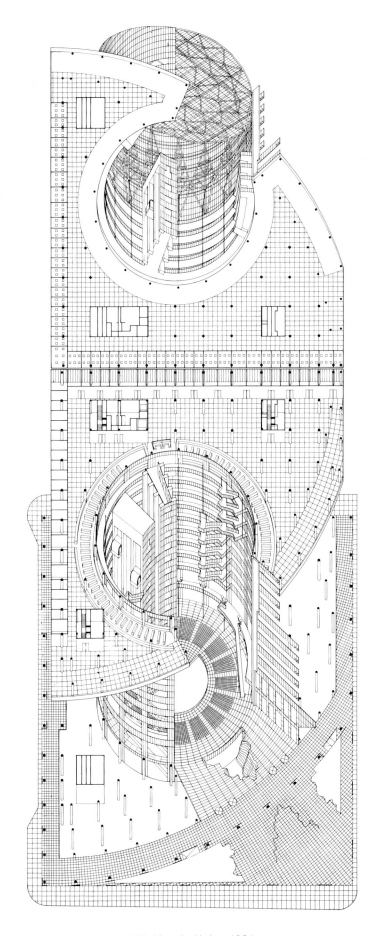

112 Murphy/Jahn 1981

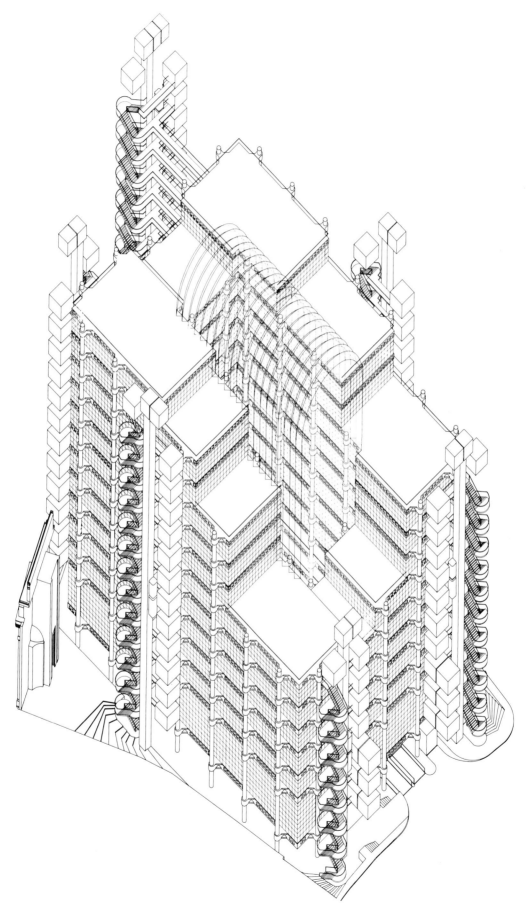

113 Richard Rogers+Partners 1979

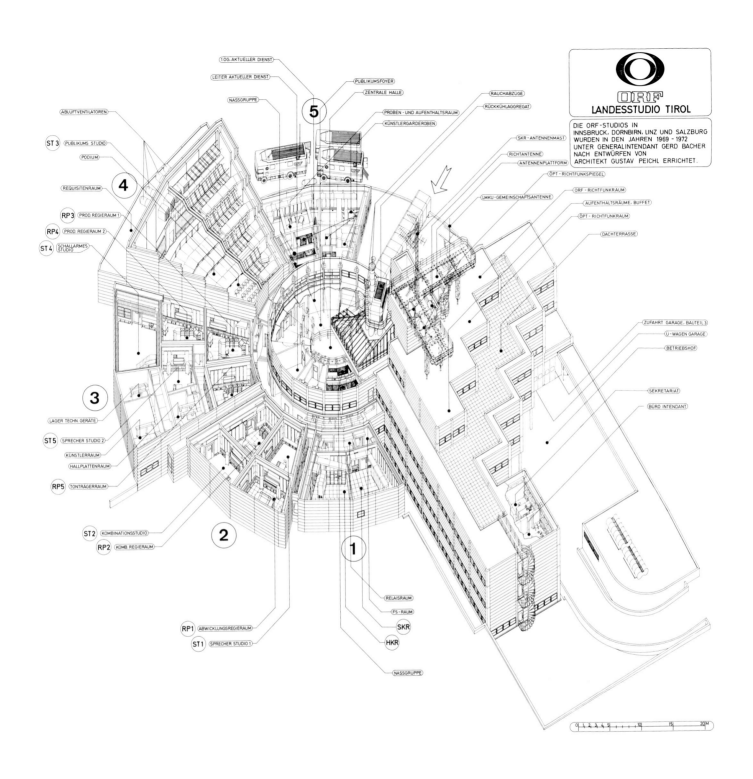

ABLUFTVENTILATOREN

ST 3 — PUBLIKUMS STUDIO
PODIUM
REQUISITENRAUM

4

RP3 — PROD. REGIERAUM 1
RP4 — PROD. REGIERAUM 2
ST 4 — SCHALLARMES STUDIO

3

LAGER TECHN. GERÄTE
ST 5 — SPRECHER STUDIO 2
KÜNSTLERRAUM
HALLPLATTENRAUM
RP5 — TONTRÄGERRAUM

ST 2 — KOMBINATIONSSTUDIO
RP2 — KOMB. REGIERAUM

2

RP1 — ABWICKLUNGSREGIERAUM
ST 1 — SPRECHER STUDIO 1

1OG. AKTUELLER DIENST
LEITER AKTUELLER DIENST
NASSGRUPPE

5

PUBLIKUMSFOYER
ZENTRALE HALLE
PROBEN · UND AUFENTHALTSRAUM
KÜNSTLERGARDEROBEN

RAUCHABZÜGE
RÜCKKÜHLAGGREGAT

SKR · ANTENNENMAST
RICHTANTENNE
ANTENNENPLATTFORM
ÖPT · RICHTFUNKSPIEGEL
ORF · RICHTFUNKRAUM
LMKU · GEMEINSCHAFTSANTENNE
AUFENTHALTSRÄUME, BUFFET
ÖPT · RICHTFUNKRAUM
DACHTERRASSE

ZUFAHRT GARAGE, BAUTEIL 3
U · WAGEN GARAGE
BETRIEBSHOF

SEKRETARIAT
BÜRO INTENDANT

1

RELAISRAUM
FS · RAUM
SKR
HKR
NASSGRUPPE

ORF
LANDESSTUDIO TIROL

DIE ORF-STUDIOS IN
INNSBRUCK, DORNBIRN, LINZ UND SALZBURG
WURDEN IN DEN JAHREN 1969 - 1972
UNTER GENERALINTENDANT GERD BACHER
NACH ENTWÜRFEN VON
ARCHITEKT GUSTAV PEICHL ERRICHTET.

0 1 2 3 4 5   10   15   20 M

114 Gustav Peichl 1969

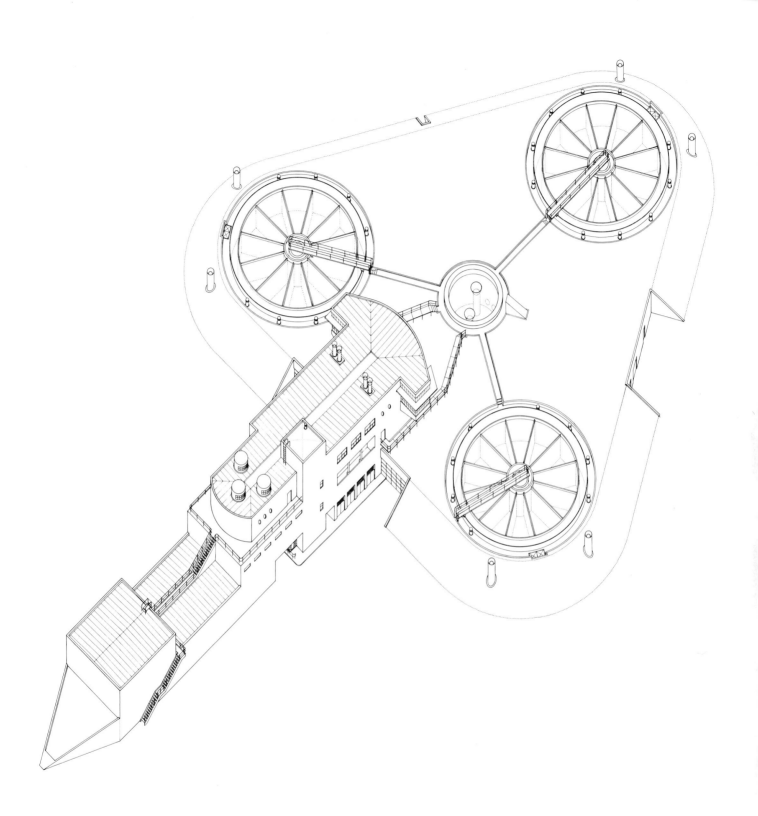

115 Gustav Peichl 1980

Flight from everything historical can no more bring salvation than a purely decorative return to forms from the past. ...
We cannot do without the past in solving the architectural problems of our own day. We may dispense with the externals, but not with the work done in the past on the mastery of tectonic problems.

In spite of all the constructional achievements and changes, most of the best building materials are still the same and many of the constructions of the past remain unsurpassed. We are absolutely compelled to stay firmly planted on the shoulders of our forefathers and we deprive ourselves of a solid foothold if we begin *needlessly* to experiment afresh on our own account. ...

The right kind of architecture is already beginning to appear, especially in the case of buildings presenting few complications; here the path of unaffected artistic expression is already being trod. It is time to stop trying to make a style of this, to stop burdening the artist with the demand to evolve an intrusive personal note, which drives him to superficialities. For the time being we must demand only *unrelenting objectivity and a solution, in keeping with good taste, of a clearly thought out problem.*

Hans Poelzig, 1906 [25]

We want it to be approximately neither straight nor crooked, neither clever nor stupid, we want it to be neither rough nor smooth, it should be all these at once. But of everything we can only have the very essence or what is most important, and in order to find this in the most correct way we shall have to be very thorough everywhere. Nothing will stand in our way more than superficiality, we shall have to keep telling ourselves: if it must be, then very little, but at least on any account thorough ...

The most important forming element for order is uniformity, and just as a flourishing arts and crafts work encourages order, it also encourages or shapes the uniform.

Our finer formative forces can unfold in work that is on purpose uniform. They would fail if faced with the entirely new. That is the benefit which the acknowledgment of order or of uniformity brings for all simple talent.

If we are to cope with our world in uniformity or even recognise it, we must necessarily direct our senses to fine particulars. ...

The more we acknowledge uniformity in our work or the less we demand that as a whole our work should be new, the more refined it will need to be. ...

Simplicity sometimes seems to be related to poverty, but in fact they have as yet little in common. Our simplicity can just as easily be great richness as our variety great poverty. ...

The ornament or the ornamental is everywhere, but its quality will be the better the less we strive for it, and it will be the more appealing the more indifferently we handle it. In our work it is roughly what idiom is in language – an inevitable component, something which emerges through living together, but something which we should not place too much weight on if we do not want it to become unpleasant.

Heinrich Tessenow, 1916 [26]

The history of a people tells of its destinies, and out of history tradition rises which brings responsibility. Those who infringe the deep meaning of tradition commit a sin against history and hence the very roots of the people.

Paul Schmitthenner, 1933 [27]

... must a form be rejected because it has been used so and so often in a banal or incomprehending way? Or is it not rather that those traditional forms which seem artifical today are bound to be discarded, while traditional forms which can be meaningfully combined with modern construction methods and needs can be used until they are replaced by better ones? Need vault construction necessarily be discarded, simply because it is not a thing of our time, if we have the financial means to use it? It has played a dominant part for more than 2000 years in the architecture of every age and every country. ...

The concept of beauty is not something that can be explained. Only the voice of our blood can give us an answer, and if we listen carefully to this voice we shall develop a sure sense of what is beautiful.

German Bestelmeyer, 1934 [28]

Architects can no longer afford to be intimidated by the puritanically moral language of orthodox Modern architecture. I like elements which are hybrid rather than "pure", compromising rather than "clean", distorted rather than "straightforward", ambiguous rather than "articulated", perverse as well as impersonal, boring as well as "interesting", conventional rather than "designed", accommodating rather than excluding, redundant rather than simple, vestigial as well as innovating, inconsistent and equivocal rather than direct and clear. I am for messy vitality over obvious unity. I include the non sequitur and proclaim the duality.

I am for richness of meaning rather than clarity of meaning; for the implicit function as well as the explicit function. I prefer "both-and" to "either-or", black and white, and sometimes gray, to black or white. A valid architecture evokes many levels of meaning and combinations of focus: its space and its elements become readable and workable in several ways at once.

But an architecture of complexity and contradiction has a special obligation toward the whole: its truth must be in its totality or its implications of totality. It must embody the difficult unity of inclusion rather than the easy unity of exclusion. More is not less.

Robert Venturi, 1968 [29]

116 Paul Bonatz 1915

117 Heinrich Tessenow 1908

118 Heinrich Tessenow 1910

119 Marcello Piacentini, Gaetano Rapisardi, Angiolo Mazzoni 1927

120 Gunnar Asplund 1921

121 Auguste Perret, Gustave Perret 1922

122 Buchman and Kahn 1930

123 Eliel Saarinen 1923

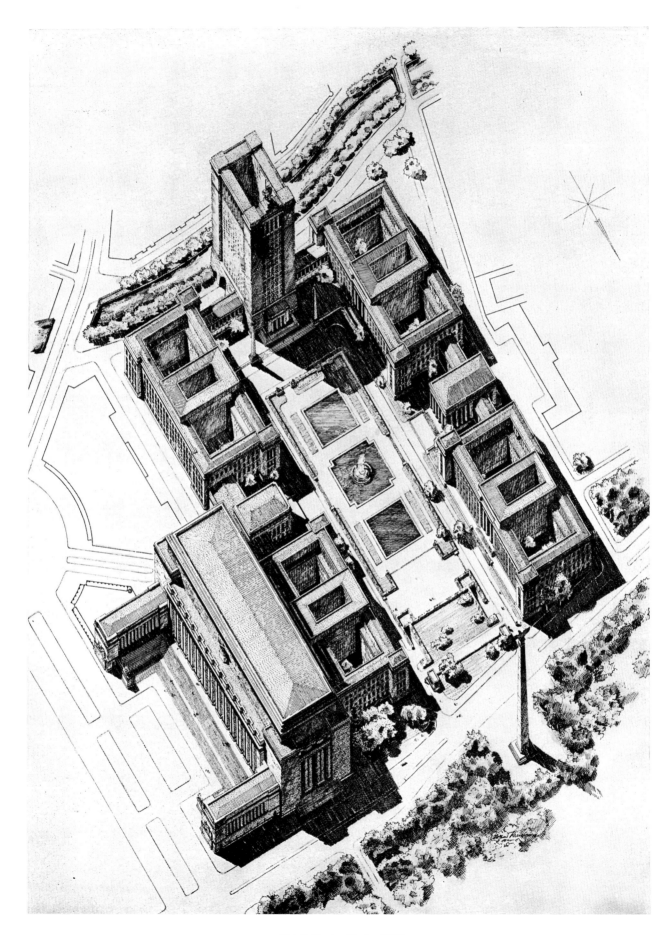

124 Wilhelm Kreis 1938

125 Philip Johnson 1958

126 Johnson/Burgee 1981

127 Venturi, Rauch and Scott Brown 1977

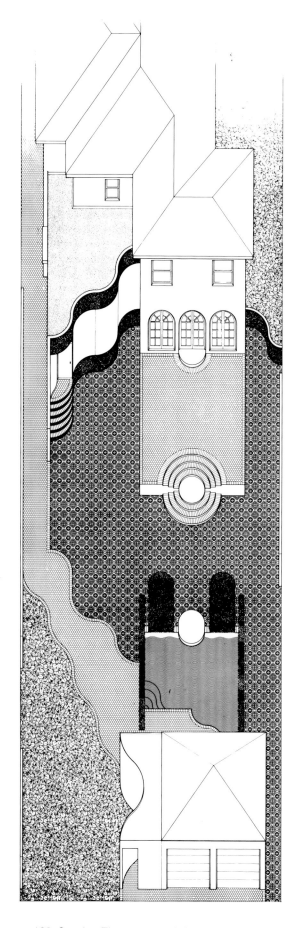

128 Stanley Tigerman and Associates 1977

129 Moore, Grover, Harper 1974

130 Moore, Grover, Harper 1979

LIVING ROOM

DINING ROOM

ENTRY HALL

BACK PORCH

131 Robert Stern 1980

150

132 Michael Graves 1978

133 Michael Graves 1979

134 Michael Graves 1980

135 Hans Hollein 1980

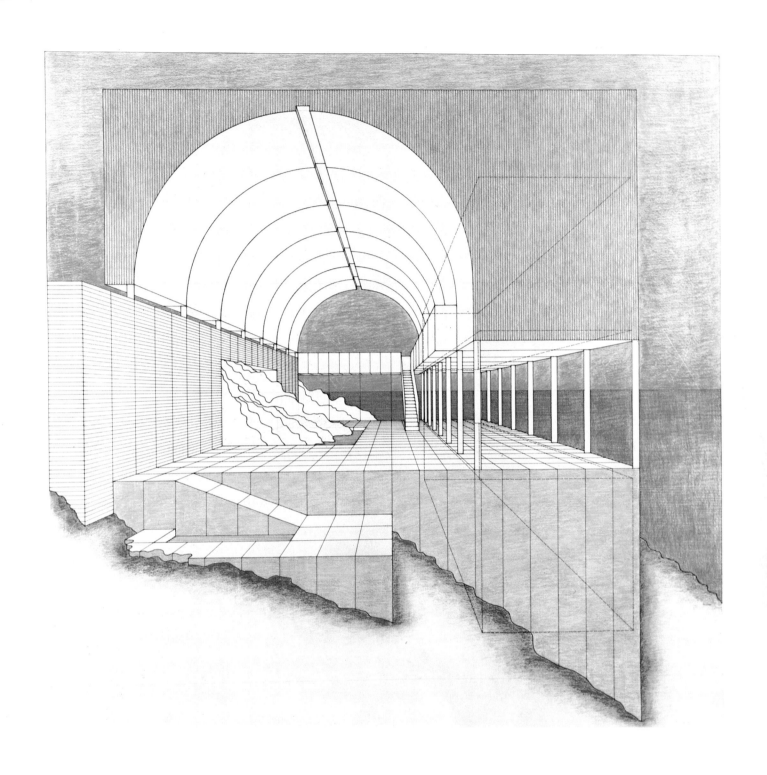

136 Friedrich St. Florian (1973–76)

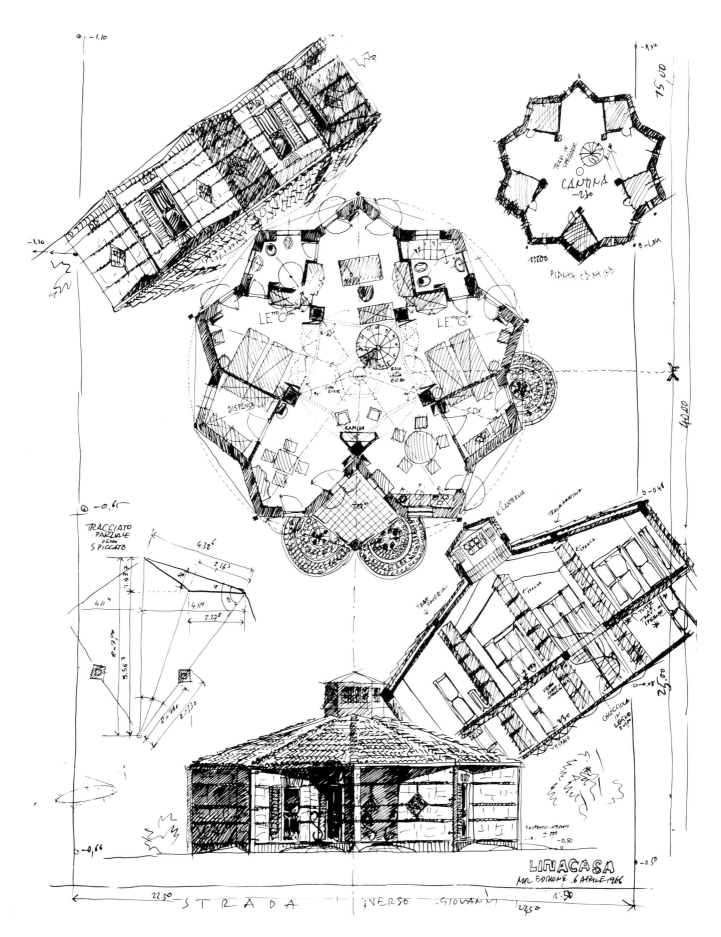

137 Mario Ridolfi 1966

138 Paolo Portoghesi 1978

157

139 James Stirling, Michael Wilford and Associates 1980

140 Taller de Arquitectura/Ricardo Bofill 1980

Design is form-making in order
Form emerges out of a system of construction
Growth is a construction
In order is creative force
In design is the means – where with what when with how much ...
Order does not imply Beauty
     The same order created the dwarf and Adonis
Design is not making Beauty
     Beauty emerges from selection
          affinities
          integration
          love
Art is a form making life in order – psychic
Order is intangible
     It is a level of creative consciousness
     forever becoming higher in level
     The higher the order the more diversity in design
Order supports integration
From what the space wants to be the unfamiliar may be revealed to the architect.
From order he will derive creative force and power of self criticism to give form to this unfamiliar.
Beauty will evolve

Louis Kahn, 1960

Architecture is a spiritual order, realized through building.
Architecture – an idea built into infinite space, manifesting man's spiritual energy and power, the material form and expression of his destiny, of his life. From its origins until today the essence and meaning of architecture have not changed. To build is a basic human need. It is first manifested not in the putting up of protective roofs, but in the erection of sacred structures, in the indication of focal points of human activity –the beginning of the city.
All building is religious.
Architecture – the expression of man himself – at once flesh and spirit.
Architecture is elemental, sensual, primitive, brutal, terrible, mighty, dominating.
But it is also the embodiment of the most subtle emotions, a sensitive record of the most refined sensations, a materialization of the spiritual.

Hans Hollein, 1962[31]

To speak of rationalism in architecture – and so to speak of reason, forms and the techniques at its disposal, etc. – means to primarily come back to the problem of knowledge: in the case of architecture this means to refer to the scientific basis of architecture itself. It is the equivalent of confirming that there is only a science of architecture in time, which has to unite in one continuous process the study of the past and of the present. ...
Precisely because of the significance which is attributed to the analysis and to the problem of knowledge, because of the particular significance which in such cases the process of research into the expression of constant or general elements assumes, through the coincidence of analysis and planning, architecture is seen in the rationalist theory especially in its

character of "building", that is as a process according to a logical order of successive selections, that is in its logical-syntactical character.
It is well known that the concept of a formal theory is linked to this, whereby the term "formal" is used not in the sense of referring to the forms of architecture but to its types and the order in which they are manifest. We therefore say that the attention of the research of rationalist thought is aimed, on theoretical level, towards the construction of a formal theory of architectural forms. This will be manifest in the examination of some exemplary types of treatises.
It is therefore evident that this is a limited selection in comparison with all those factors contributing to the complexity of the achievements of man. It nevertheless corresponds to that demand of constant and sure elements which characterises this direction of selection. It is therefore a deliberate selection, based upon a precise concept of the "significance" of architecture, a precise idea of architecture and the project vis à vis of the experience of architecture in time.

Giorgio Grassi, 1967[32]

Against the anti-historicism of the modern movement we repropose the study of the history of the city. The narrow rationalism of modern architecture is expanded to understand the city in all its typological components. The history of architectural and urban culture is seen as the history of types. Types of settlements, types of spaces (public and private), types of buildings, types of construction. The bourgeois concept of architectural history – basically concerned with the monument – is extended to include the typological complexity of the urban fabric, of the anonymous buildings forming the flesh of the city, the skin of its public space. The buildings which are not so much the result of high art but of building tradition. ...
The "Art of Building Cities" has to find its way into legislation. The complex architectural scheme, precise types of urban space (*streets, avenues, squares, arcades, colonnades*) will have to replace the two-dimensional zoning spaces. A functionally complex and visually simple spatial continuum has to replace the contemporary system of disintegrated functions and buildings; inside a precise relationship of building-typology and morphology of urban spaces, we re-establish a dialectic of public buildings (monuments) and urban fabric.

Leon Krier, 1978[33]

141 Louis Kahn 1960

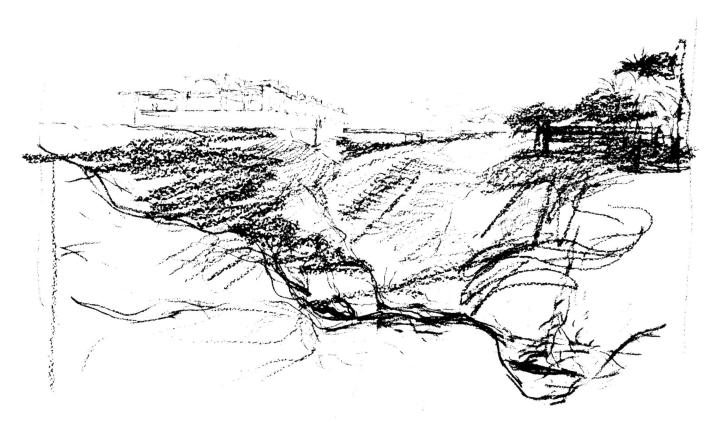

142 Louis Kahn (1959–65)

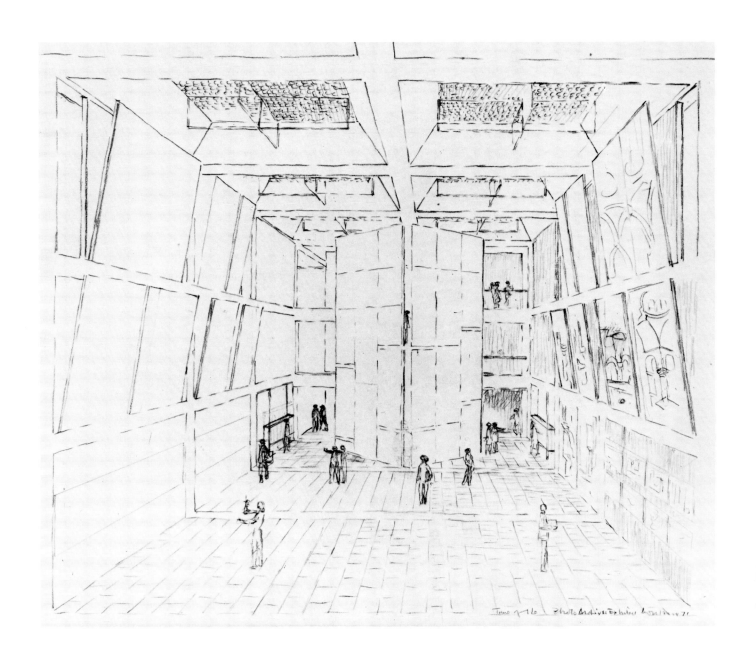

143 Louis Kahn 1971

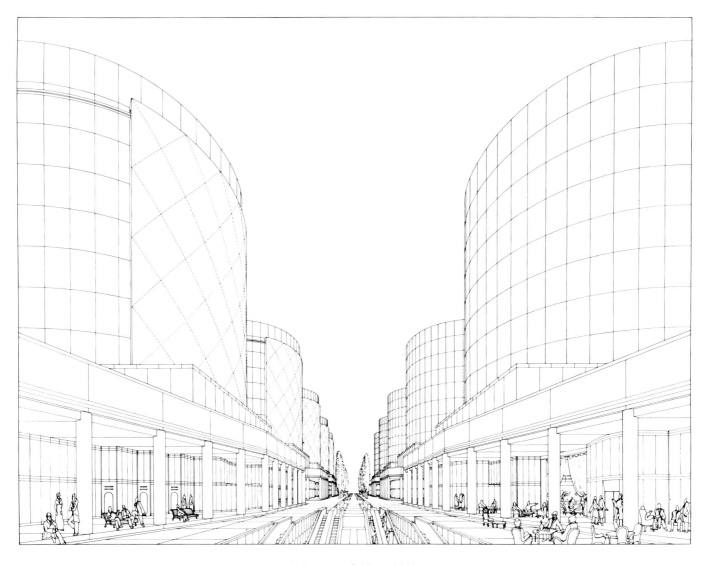

144 James Stirling 1969

145 James Stirling 1970

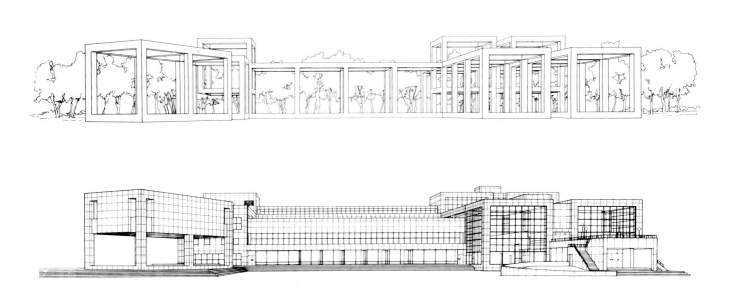

146 Arata Isozaki 1976

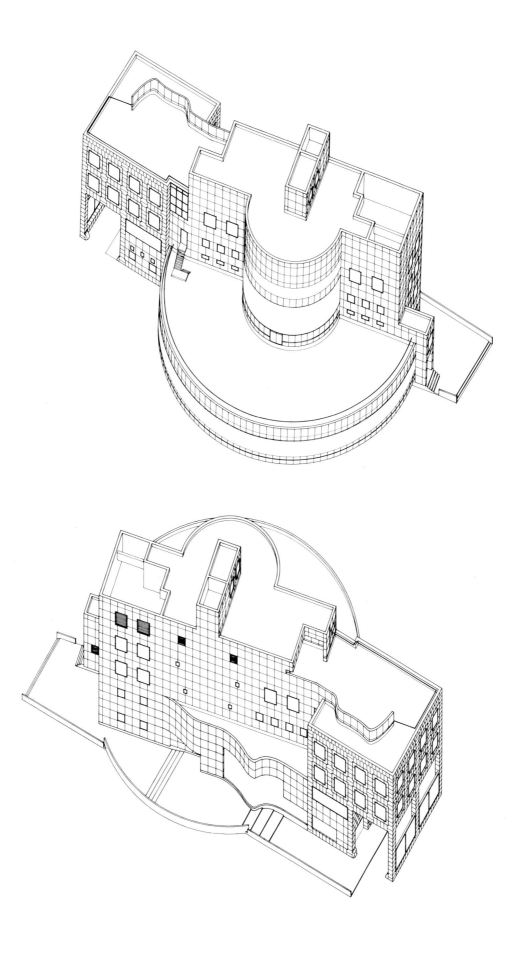

147 Arata Isozaki 1978

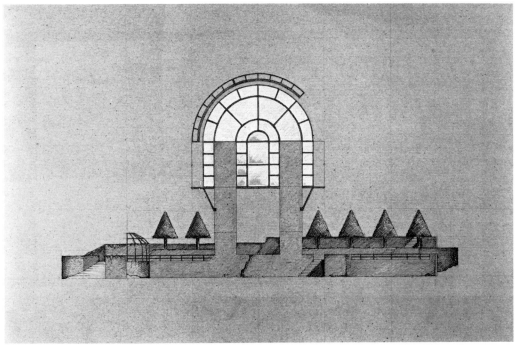

148 + 149 Josef Paul Kleihues 1972

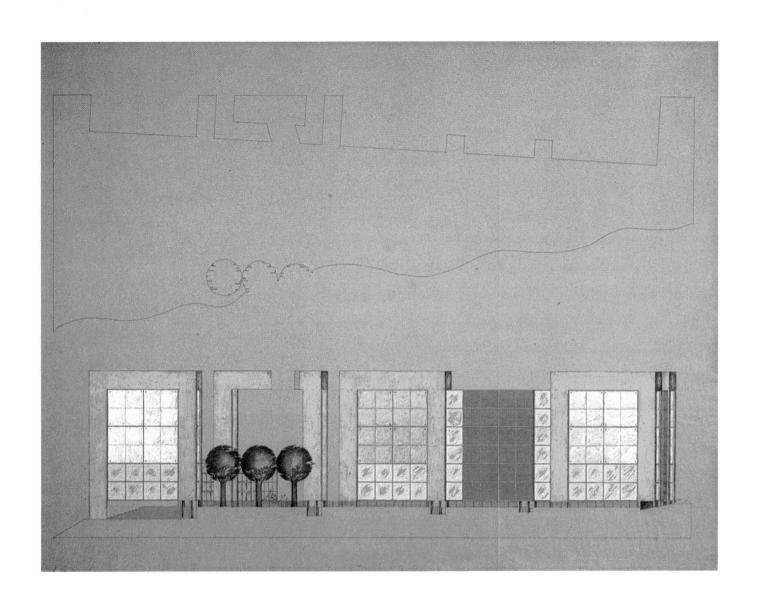

150 Josef Paul Kleihues 1975

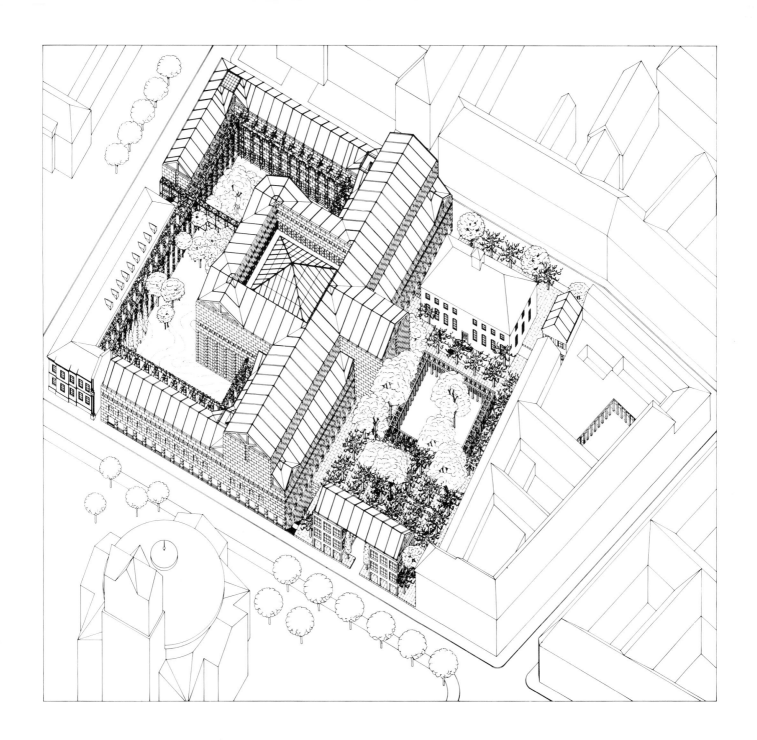

151 Oswald Mathias Ungers 1979

152 Oswald Mathias Ungers 1980

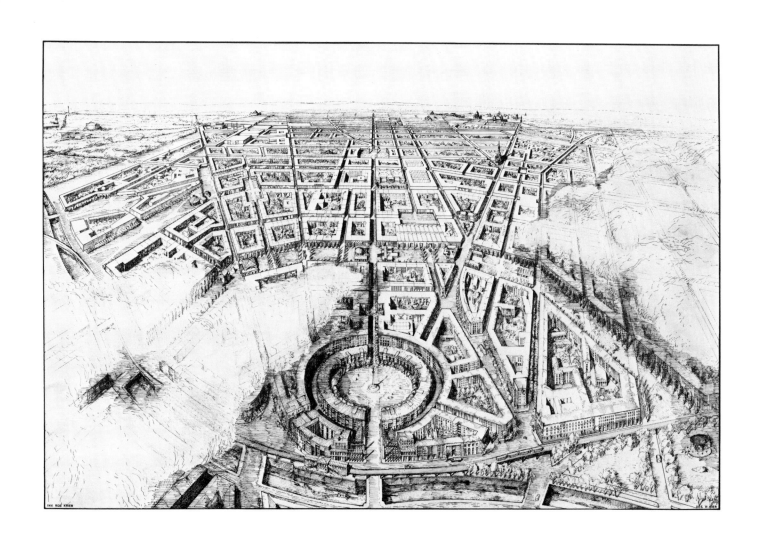

153 Rob Krier 1977

154 Rob Krier 1980

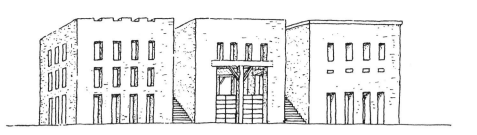

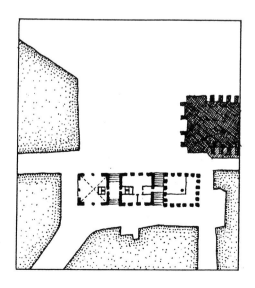

155 Leon Krier 1975

156 Leon Krier 1977

175

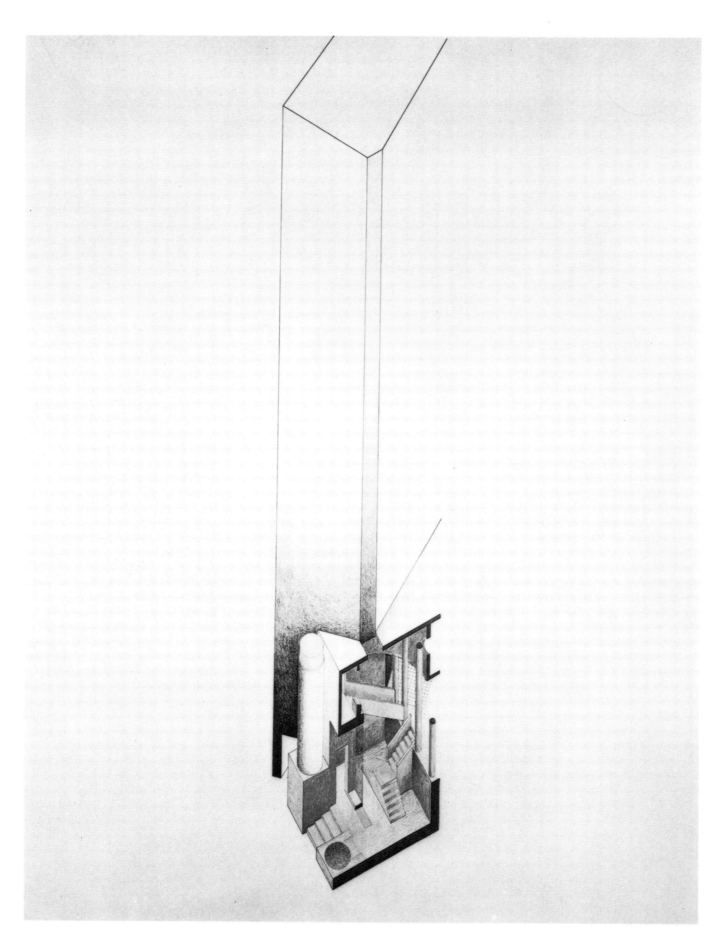

157 Diana Agrest, Mario Gandelsonas 1977

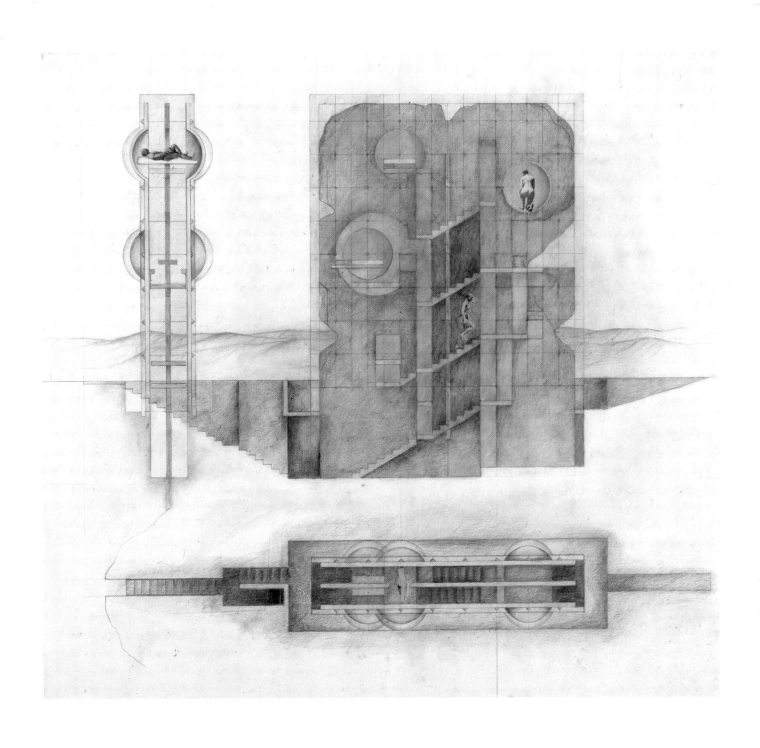

158 Raimund Abraham 1974/75

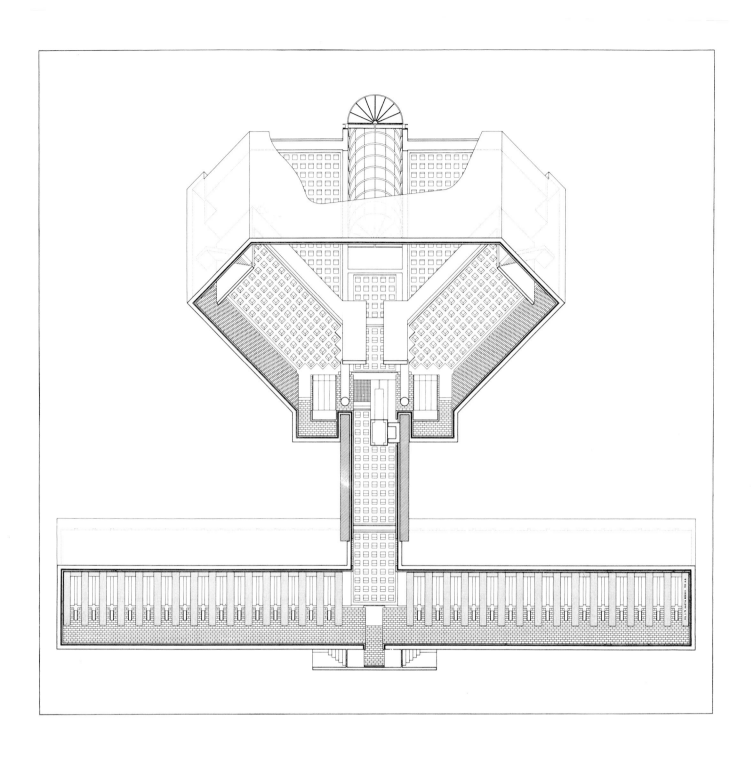

159 Mario Botta 1979

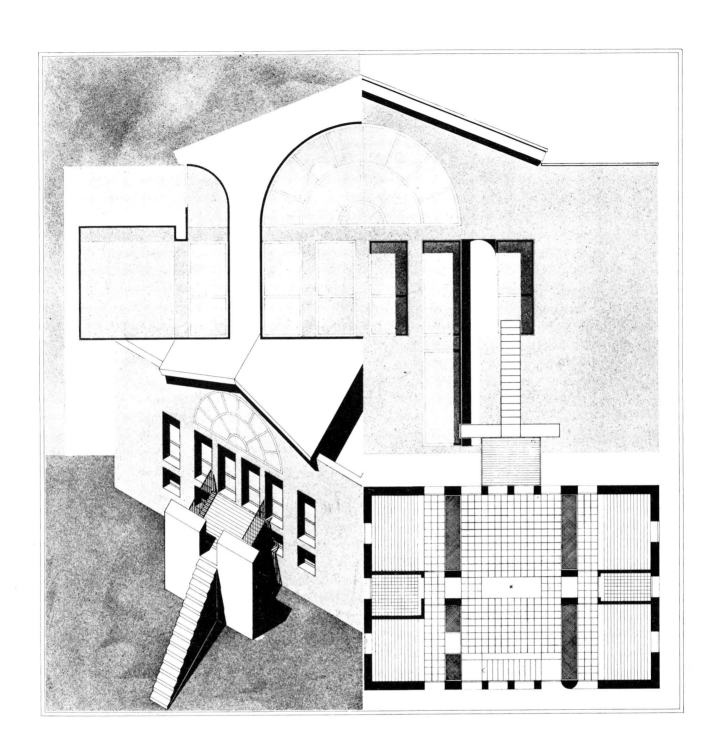

160 Bruno Reichlin, Fabio Reinhart 1975

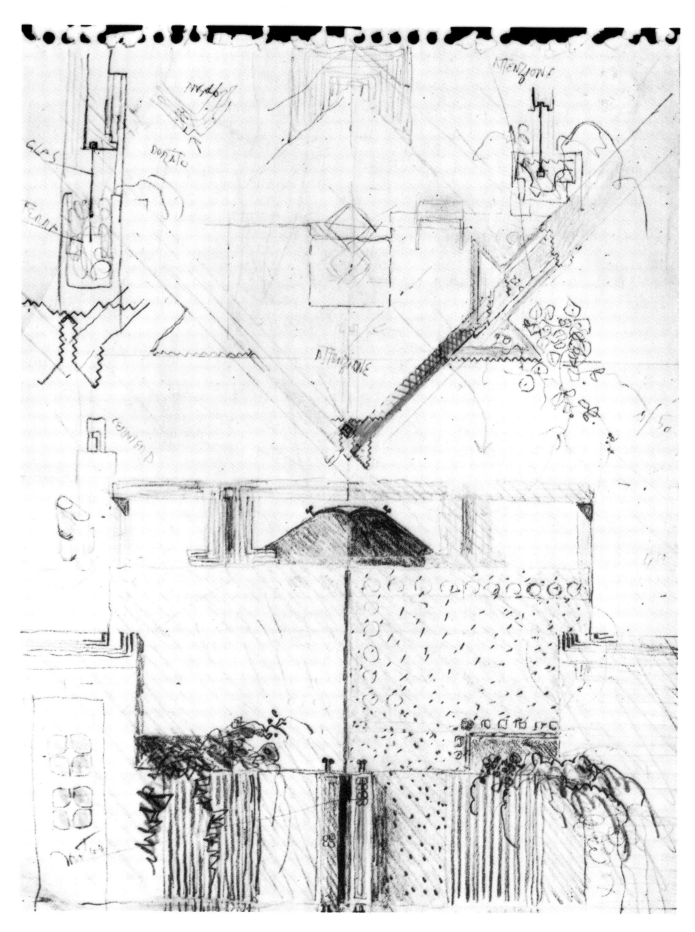

161 Carlo Scarpa (1969–75)

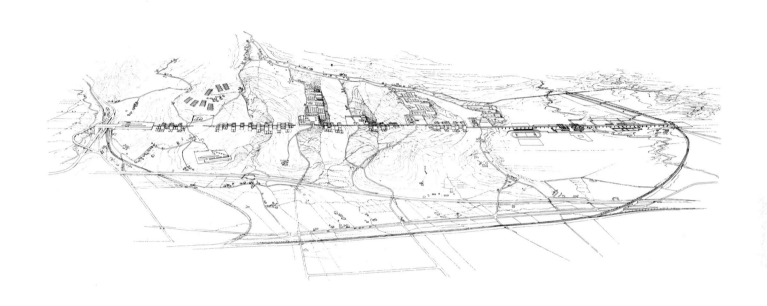

162 Gregotti Associati 1973

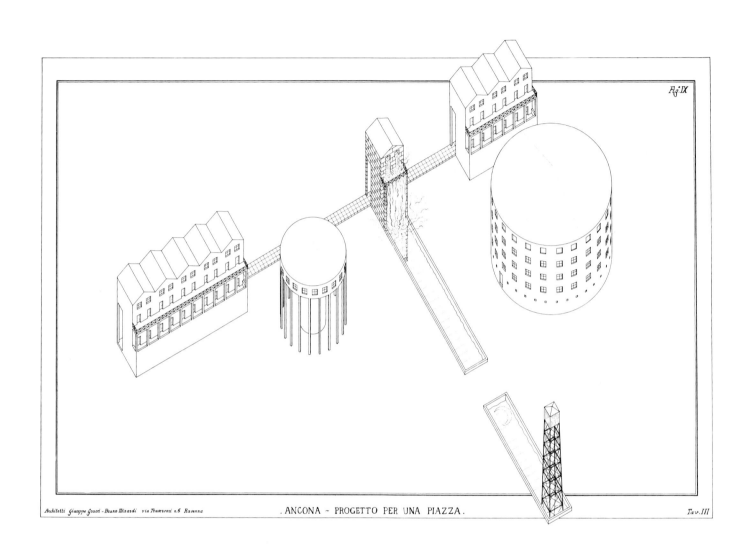

Fig. IX

Architetti Giuseppe Grossi - Bruno Minardi via Traversari n.6 Ravenna   . ANCONA ~ PROGETTO PER UNA PIAZZA .   Tav. III

163 Giuseppe Grossi, Bruno Minardi 1977/78

164 Rodolfo Machado, Jorge Silvetti 1979

183

166 Giorgio Grassi 1972

184

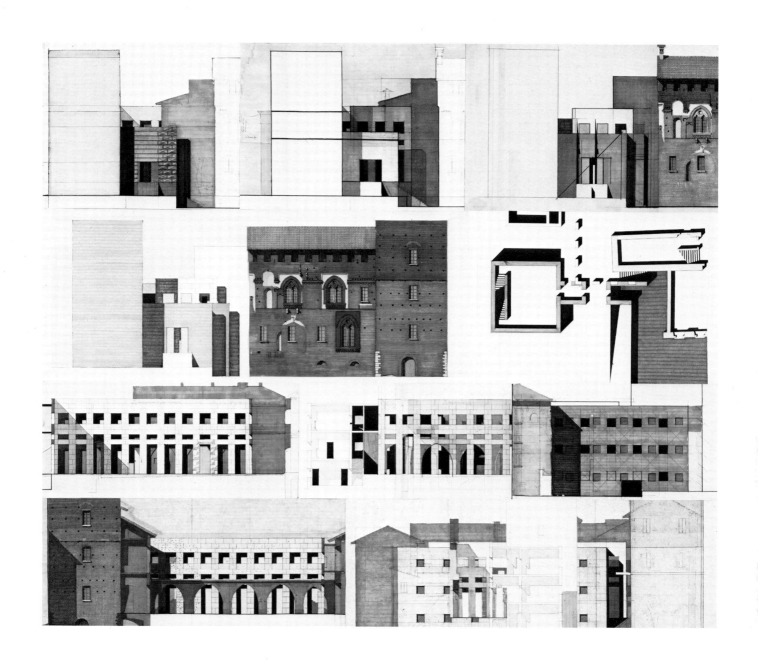

165 Giorgio Grassi 1970

185

167 Aldo Rossi 1968

186

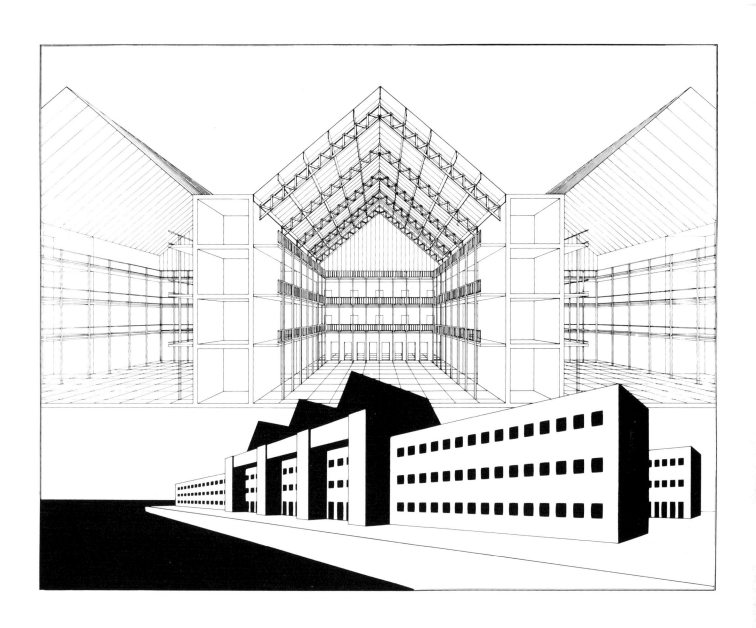

168 Aldo Rossi, Gianni Braghieri 1974

· Pages 6–17:

1 Horatio Greenough. Quoted from: Frank Lloyd Wright, *Modern Architecture,* Princeton, 1931.
2 A. Izzo and C. Gubitosi, *Frank Lloyd Wright. Drawings 1887–1959,* Florence and London, 1978.
3 Alvar Aalto, "National Planning and the Goals of Culture", lecture, 1949. Quoted from: Aarno Ruusuvuori (ed.), *Alvar Aalto 1898–1976,* Helsinki, 1978, p. 34.
4 Alvar Aalto, "Rationalism and Man", lecture at the annual meeting of the Swedish Crafts Association, 1935. Quoted from: Aarno Ruusuvuori (ed.), op. cit., p. 33.
5 Alvar Aalto, *Synopsis. Malerei, Architektur, Skulptur,* Basel and Stuttgart, 1970.
6 Hugo Häring, "Wege zur Form", *Die Form,* vol. 1 (1925), no. 1.
7 Ibid.
8 Ibid.
9 Leaflet of the Arbeitsrat für Kunst, Berlin, 1919.
10 Franco Borsi (ed.), *Hermann Finsterlin. Idea dell'architettura. Architektur in seiner Idee,* Florence, 1969.
11 Bruno Zevi, *Erich Mendelsohn. Opera completa,* Milan, 1970.
12 Erich Mendelsohn. Quoted from: Reyner Banham, *Theory and Design in the First Machine Age,* Cambridge, Mass., 1980, p. 181.
13 Erich Mendelsohn. Quoted from Reyner Banham, op. cit., p. 181.
14 Werner Hegemann, "Aus der Amsterdamer Schreckenskammer", *Wasmuths Monatshefte für Baukunst,* 1925, no. 1, pp. 147–151.
15 Luciano Caramel and Alberto Longatti, *Antonio Sant'Elia,* exhibition catalogue, Como, 1962.
16 The statement was probably not written by Sant'Elia himself, it is more likely a text by Ugo Nebbia which follows Sant'Elia's ideas. See the letter by Ugo Nebbia in the newspaper *L'Espresso* of 9 Dec. 1956. The discussion on the authorship for the statement, which of course is closely linked with the question of whether Sant'Elia belonged to the Futurist movement (and is not without polemical element considering Marinetti's later liaison with Fascism) was conducted by Giovanni Bernasconi, Bruno Zevi, Giulia Veronesi, Reyner Banham and Jörn-Peter Schmidt-Tomsen.
17 Karl and Eva Mang, *Wiener Architektur 1860–1930 in Zeichnungen,* Stuttgart, 1979. English edition: *Viennese Architecture 1860–1930 in Drawings,* New York and London, 1979.
18 Ludwig Glaeser (ed.), *Ludwig Mies van der Rohe. Drawings in the Collection of the Museum of Modern Art,* New York, 1969.
19 *Le Corbusier. Dessins, Drawings, Disegni,* Rome, 1978, and Paris, 1979. English edition: *Le Corbusier. Selected Drawings,* London, 1981.
20 Le Corbusier-Saugnier, *Vers une Architecture,* Paris, n.d. (1923), p. 25.

21 "The beginning of an architecture which is spatial and functional and which is drawn using axonometry is already apparent. This method of representation enables all the parts of the house to be read at once, in their correct proportions, even from above and below, that is without the vanishing points of perspective. In the two-dimensional representation, on the contrary, the building can be perceived by the eye directly in its cubic volume. The ground-plan is about to go and be replaced by a clearer reading-system in which the dimensions and the necessary structures will be readily apparent. Of course the whole design, from the foundations to the roof, has to be worked out axonometrically." Theo van Doesburg, "Het Bouwbedrijf", *De Stijl,* VI (1919), no. 15, pp. 305–308.
22 Theo van Doesburg, "De architectuur als synthese der nieuwe beelding", *De Stijl,* XII (1924), no. 6/7, pp. 78–83. Quoted from: Ulrich Conrads (ed.), *Programs and manifestos on 20th-century architecture,* Cambridge, Mass., 1975, pp. 78–80.
23 El Lissitzky also regarded perspective as contravening the modern artist's concept of space. "The central perspective which was developed and most widely used during the Renaissance showed the cube with one side parallel to our face. It is a view of the facade, it has the depth of a stage, and that is why perspective was so integrated with scenic design." El Lissitzky, "K. und Pangeometrie", *Europa-Almanach,* 1925, pp. 103–113.
24 See: Bruno Reichlin, in: *Alberto Sartoris,* exhibition catalogue, Zurich and Lausanne, 1978, pp. 8–25.
25 Gruppo 7, "Architettura", *Rassegna Italiana,* 1 Dec. 1926. Quoted from: Michele Cennamo, *Materiali per l'analisi dell'architettura moderna. La prima Esposizione Italiana di Architettura Razionale,* Naples, 1973, p. 39.
26 Quoted from: Bruno Reichlin, op. cit., p. 9.
27 As Bruno Reichlin remarked, a passage in the obituary which Sartoris wrote for van Doesburg has autobiographical significance and it illustrates the basic essence of his own work better than any commentary by any other writer: "I always thought that Theo van Doesburg loved architecture like an aristocrat of thought: this means that he was both enthusiastic and disdainful of it at once. He was enthusiastic about the work he was about to create and disdainful of the created work. It was for this reason that he was able so quickly (through the discipline of selection which he learned from the rigorous doctrine of neo-plastic painting) to assemble with such prodigious energy the plastic and constructive elements of his new spatial architecture." Alberto Sartoris, "Pour Theo van Doesburg", *Werk,* vol. XVIII (1931), no. 9, p. XXXIV. Quoted from: Bruno Reichlin, op. cit., p. 10.
28 *Five Architects,* New York, 1972.
29 Peter Eisenman, "Le rappresentazioni del dubbio: nel segno del segno", *Rassegna,* 1982, no. 9, pp. 69–74.

30 Peter Eisenman, *a + u. Architecture and Urbanism,* no. 123 (1980), p. 98.
31 *John Hejduk,* exhibition catalogue, Zurich, 1973, p. 15.
32 Herbert Marcuse. Quoted from: Karin Thomas, *Kunst-Praxis heute,* Cologne, 1972, p. 179.
33 *Die Zeichnungen von Heinrich Tessenow. Der Bestand in der Kunstbibliothek Berlin,* Waltraut Strey (ed.), Berlin, 1981.
34 Hugh Ferris, *The Metropolis of To-morrow,* New York, 1929.
35 Robert A.M. Stern, "Drawing Towards a More Modern Architecture", *Architectural Design,* vol. 47 (1977), no. 6, pp. 382, 383. The whole issue is devoted to the subject of architectural drawing in the USA ("AD Profiles 6. America Now: Drawing Towards a More Modern Architecture").
36 Michael Graves, "The Necessity for Drawing: Tangible Speculation", *Architectural Design,* vol. 47 (1977), no. 6, pp. 384–394. See also: "Michael Graves at the Max Protetch Gallery", *Architectural Design,* vol. 47 (1979), no. 10/11, pp. 272–277. And: "Vincent Scully on Michael Graves Monograph", ibid., p. 278.
37 Francesco Moschini (ed.), *Paolo Portoghesi. Progetti e disegni 1949–1979. Projects and Drawings 1949–1979,* Florence, 1979.
38 Annabelle d'Huart (ed.), *Ricardo Bofill, Taller de Arquitectura. Los espacios de Abraxas. El palacio, el teatro, el arco,* Paris, 1981.
39 See: Friedrich Achleitner, "Psychogramm oder Gegenwelt? Über die Rolle der Zeichnung in der Architektur und über die Rolle der Architektur in der Zeichnung Rob Kriers", *Um Bau,* no. 4, May 1981, pp. 71–77.
40 *Leon Krier. Drawings 1967–1980,* Brussels, 1980.
41 *Raimund Abraham. Collisions,* exhibition catalogue, New Haven, Connecticut, 1981.
42 Daniel Libeskind, "Wider die altehrwürdige 'Sprache der Architektur'", *Daidalos,* no. 1 (1981), pp. 96–102.
43 Massimo Scolari, "Considerazioni e aforismi sul disegno", *Rassegna,* 1982, no. 9, pp. 79–85. Francesco Moschini (ed.), *Massimo Scolari, Acquerelli e disegni 1965–1980. Watercolors and drawings 1965–1980,* Florence, 1980.
44 *Arduino Cantafora, Le stagioni delle Case. La Casa del Sole Nascente e l'annesso Ospedale di St. James,* Rome, 1980.
45 *Giuseppe Grossi, Bruno Minardi, Elementi, Edifici, Progetti,* Rome, 1981.
46 *Franco Purini. Alcune forme della casa,* Rome, 1979.
47 Italo Rota (ed.), *Mario Botta. Architetture e progetti negli anni '70. Architecture and projects in the '70s,* Milan, 1979.
48 *Giorgio Grassi. Progetti e disegni 1965–1980,* exhibition catalogue, Mantua, 1982.
49 Francesco Moschini (ed.), *Aldo Rossi. Progetti e disegni 1962–1979. Projects and drawings 1962–1979,* Florence, 1979.
50 See: Franco Rella, *Il silenzio e le parole. Il pensiero nel tempo della crisi,* Milan, 1981.

51 "Dieses ist lange her/Ora questo é perduto". Engraving by Aldo Rossi, 1975. See also: Paul Katzberger and Dietmar Steiner, "'… Dieses ist lange her …', Bemerkungen zu Aldo Rossi", *Um Bau,* no. 1, December 1979, pp. 18–30.
52 Ludwig Mies van der Rohe, inaugural address as Director of Architecture at Armour Institute of Technology in Chicago, 1938. Quoted from: Philip C. Johnson, *Mies van der Rohe,* New York, 1953, pp. 196–200.
53 Ibid.

Pages 18–187:

1 Frank Lloyd Wright, "Die Souveränität des Einzelnen" ("The Sovereignty of the Individual"), preface to: Frank Lloyd Wright, *Ausgeführte Bauten und Entwürfe,* Berlin, 1910. Quoted from: *Frank Lloyd Wright: Writings and Buildings,* New York, 1960, pp. 84–106.
2 Frank Lloyd Wright, "To the Young Man in Architecture", lecture at Princeton University, 1930. Quoted from: *Frank Lloyd Wright: Writings and Buildings,* loc. cit., pp. 232–251.
3 Hugo Häring, "Das Haus als organhaftes Gebilde", *Innendekoration,* vol. 37 (1932). Quoted from: Ulrich Conrads (ed.), *Programs and manifestos on 20th-century architecture,* Cambridge, Mass., 1975, pp. 126, 127.
4 Alvar Aalto, "Rationalism and Man", lecture at the annual meeting of the Swedish Crafts Association, 1935. Quoted from: Aarno Ruusuvuori (ed.), *Alvar Aalto 1898–1976,* Helsinki, 1978.
5 Alvar Aalto, "The Influence of Constructions and Materials on Modern Architecture", lecture, 1938. Quoted from: Aarno Ruusuvuori (ed.), op. cit.
6 Alvar Aalto, "National Planning and the Goals of Culture", 1949. Quoted from: Aarno Ruusuvuori (ed.), op. cit.
7 Walter Gropius, "Der Neue Baugedanke", leaflet to the "Ausstellung für unbekannte Architekten", Berlin, 1919. Quoted from: Ulrich Conrads (ed.), op. cit., pp. 46, 47.
8 Bruno Taut, "Nieder der Seriosismus!", *Frühlicht,* 1920, no. 1. Quoted from: Ulrich Conrads (ed.), op. cit. pp. 57, 58.
9 Erich Mendelsohn, "Dynamik und Funktion", lecture, 1923. Quoted from: Ulrich Conrads (ed.), op. cit., pp. 72, 73.
10 Hermann Finsterlin, "Casa nova", *Wendingen,* 1924, no. 3. Quoted from: Ulrich Conrads (ed.), op. cit., pp. 83–86.
11 Bernhard Hoetger, "Weltbauen", 1928. Quoted from: Ulrich Conrads (ed.), op. cit., pp. 107, 108.
12 Frederick Kiesler, in: *Le Surréalisme en 1947,* Paris, 1947, pp. 131 ff. Quoted from: Ulrich Conrads (ed.), op. cit., pp. 150, 151.
13 Adolf Loos, "Ornament und Verbrechen", 1908. Quoted from: Ulrich Conrads (ed.), op. cit., pp. 19–24.
14 (Antonio Sant'Elia), "L'architettura futurista", *Lacerba,* July 1914. Quoted from: Ulrich Conrads (ed.), op. cit., pp. 34–38.
15 Le Corbusier-Saugnier, *Vers une architecture,* Paris, n.d. (1923), pp. 16, 116. Quoted from: Le Corbusier, *Towards a New Architecture,* London, 1946, pp. 31, 135, 138.
16 Gruppo 7, "Architettura", *Rassegna Italiana,* December 1926 till May 1927. Quoted from: Michele Cennamo, *Materiali per l'analisi dell' architettura moderna. La prima Esposizione Italiana di Architettura Razionale,* Naples, 1973, pp. 40, 41.
17 Ludwig Mies van der Rohe, inaugural address as Director of Architecture at Armour Institute of Technology in Chicago, 1938. Quoted from: Philip C. Johnson, *Mies van der Rohe,* New York, 1953, pp. 196–200.

18 Peter Eisenman, "Cardboard Architecture: House I", 1969. Quoted from: *Five Architects,* New York, 1975, pp. 15–17.
19 (Antonio Sant'Elia), "L'architettura futurista", loc. cit. Quoted from: Ulrich Conrads (ed.), op. cit., pp. 34–38.
20 Ludwig Mies van der Rohe, address to the Institute of Technology in Chicago, 1950. Quoted from: Philip C. Johnson, op. cit., pp. 203, 204.
21 Konrad Wachsmann, "Sieben Thesen", *Baukunst und Werkform,* vol. 10 (1957), no. 1. Quoted from: Ulrich Conrads (ed.), op. cit., p. 156.
22 Warren Chalk, "Archigram 1970–71", *Architectural Design,* vol. XLI, August 1971. Quoted from: Philip Drew, *Third Generation. The Changing Meaning of Architecture,* New York and London, 1972, p. 103.
23 Laurids Ortner, *Provisorische Architektur – Medium der Stadtgestaltung,* Düsseldorf, 1976, p. 11.
24 Coop Himmelblau, *Architektur muß brennen,* Graz, 1980.
25 Hans Poelzig, essay on the "Dritte Deutsche Kunstgewerbe-Ausstellung Dresden 1906", 1906. Quoted from: Ulrich Conrads (ed.), op. cit., pp. 14–17.
26 Heinrich Tessenow. *Hausbau und dergleichen,* Berlin, 1916.
27 Paul Schmitthenner, "Tradition und Neues Bauen", *Deutsche Kulturwacht,* 1933, no. 17.
28 German Bestelmeyer, "Baukunst und Gegenwart", *Zentralblatt der Bauverwaltung,* 1934, no. 17.
29 Robert Venturi, *Complexity and Contradiction in Architecture,* New York, 1966, pp. 22, 23.
30 Louis I. Kahn, "Order is", *Perspecta,* no. 3 (1960).
31 Hans Hollein, 1962. Quoted from: Ulrich Conrads (ed.), op. cit., pp. 181, 182.
32 Giorgio Grassi, *La costruzione logica dell'architettura,* Padua, 1967, pp. 27, 28.
33 Leon Krier, "The Reconstruction of the City", in: *Rational Architecture/Architecture Rationelle,* Brussels, 1978, pp. 38–42.

78 Theo van Doesburg. Counter-construction. 1923. Phototype with gouache. $22\frac{1}{2} \times 22\frac{1}{2}''$. Collection of N. van Doesburg, Meudon.

79 Willem Marinus Dudok. Town hall in Hilversum. 1924. Pencil. Nederlands Documentatiecentrum voor de Bouwkunst, Amsterdam.

80 Willem Marinus Dudok. Town hall in Hilversum. 1924. Pencil. $15\frac{1}{2} \times 20\frac{3}{8}''$. Nederlands Documentatiecentrum voor de Bouwkunst, Amsterdam.

81 Rudolf Schindler. The Play Mart, Los Angeles. 1921. Pencil, ink, gouache and watercolours. $19\frac{3}{4} \times 8\frac{7}{8}''$. University Art Museum, University of California, Santa Barbara.

82 Richard Neutra. Rush City Reformed. Approx. 1927. Pencil. $12 \times 16''$. Neutra Archive, University of California, Los Angeles.

83 Paul Rudolph. Art and Architecture Building, Yale University, New Haven, Connecticut. 1958. Pencil and ink. $36 \times 48''$.

84 Paul Rudolph. Callahan House, Birmingham, Alabama. 1965. Ink.

85 Cesar Pelli & Associates. The Long Gallery House. Draughtsman: Bradford Fiske. 1980. $36 \times 24''$.

86 Cesar Pelli & Associates. Extension and air-rights addition to the Museum of Modern Art, New York. Draughtsman: Diana Balmori. 1977. Coloured pencils. $66\frac{1}{8} \times 48''$.

87 James Stirling and James Gowan. Leicester University Engineering Building. Draughtsman: James Stirling. 1959. Ink. $14 \times 12''$.

88 James Stirling. Cambridge University History Building. 1964. Ink. $11 \times 8''$.

89 Richard Meier & Partners. The Atheneum, New Harmony, Indiana. Draughtsman: Steven Forman. 1979. Ink and watercolours. $16\frac{5}{8} \times 24\frac{1}{2}''$.

90 Richard Meier & Partners. The Atheneum, New Harmony, Indiana. 1976. Ink.

91 Richard Meier & Partners. Arts and Crafts Museum, Frankfurt am Main. Draughtsman: Steven Forman. 1979. Ink. $39\frac{3}{8} \times 39\frac{3}{8}''$.

92 Michael Graves. Hanselman House, Fort Wayne, Indiana. 1969. Ink.

93 Peter Eisenman. House III (Miller House, Lakeville, Connecticut). Built in 1969/70. Ink.

94 Peter Eisenman. House El Even Odd (Forster House, Palo Alto, California). 1978. Ink.

95 John Hejduk. One Half House. 1966. Ink.

96 Charles Gwathmey. House in Bridgehampton, Long Island. 1969. Ink.

97 Oswald Mathias Ungers. Project for Roosevelt Island, New York, 1975.

98 Elia and Zoe Zenghelis/Office for Metropolitan Architecture (OMA). Hotel Sphynx, Times Square, New York. 1975. Acrylic colours. $21\frac{5}{8} \times 18\frac{1}{8}''$. Gilman Paper Co., New York.

99 Richard Buckminster Fuller. Dymaxion House. 1927.

100 Konrad Wachsmann. Vinegrape. 1953/54. $24 \times 90''$ (the original drawing is only half size). Judith Wachsmann, Los Angeles.

101 Kiyonori Kikutake. Civic hall in Hagi. 1969. Ink. $23\frac{5}{8} \times 33\frac{1}{2}''$.

102 Peter Cook. Plug-in City. 1964. Ink.

103 Peter Cook. University Node. 1965. Ink.

104 Stanley Tigerman. Instant City. 1968. Ink.

105 Günther Domenig and Eilfried Huth. Project for Ragnitz-Graz. Between 1966 and 1969.

106 Haus-Rucker-Co. Pneumacosm, New York. Draughtsman: Günter Zamp-Kelp. 1967/68.

107 Haus-Rucker-Co. Verwechslung in Basel (Confusion in Basel). Draughtsman: Günter Zamp-Kelp. 1977. Dr. Werner Audretsch, Düsseldorf.

108 Coop Himmelblau. Wolke (Cloud). 1968.

109 Coop Himmelblau. Project for a mobile pneumatic living structure. Between 1968 and 1972.

110 Foster Associates. Olsen Centre, London. Draughtsman: Birkin Haward. 1969. Ink.

111 Foster Associates. Headquarters of the Hong Kong and Shanghai Banking Corporation, Hong Kong. Draughtsman: Birkin Haward. 1981. Ink.

112 Murphy/Jahn. State of Illinois Center, Chicago. 1981. Ink. $60 \times 30''$.

113 Richard Rogers + Partners. Headquarters of the Corporation of Lloyd's Bank, London. Draughtsman: Kieran Breen. 1979. Ink.

114 Gustav Peichl. Branch station of the ORF in Innsbruck. 1969. Ink. $47\frac{1}{4} \times 59''$.

115 Gustav Peichl. Phosphate extraction plant in Berlin-Tegel. 1980. Ink. $19\frac{5}{8} \times 16\frac{1}{2}''$.

116 Paul Bonatz. War memorial. 1915.

117 Heinrich Tessenow. One-family terrace houses for workers. 1908.

118 Heinrich Tessenow. Bildungsanstalt für rhythmische Gymnastik (Jaques-Dalcroze-Institute), Hellerau, near Dresden. 1910.

119 Marcello Piacentini, Gaetano Rapisardi and Angiolo Mazzoni. Palace of the League of Nations, Geneva. 1927.

120 Gunnar Asplund. Municipal library in Stockholm. 1921.

121 Auguste and Gustave Perret. Tower blocks in the surroundings of Paris. 1922.

122 Buchman and Kahn. Skyscraper. Draughtsman: Ely Jacques Kahn. 1930. Pencil. $22\frac{1}{4} \times 13\frac{1}{2}''$. Cooper-Hewitt Museum, New York.

123 Eliel Saarinen. Grant Hotel, Chicago. 1923. Pencil.

124 Wilhelm Kreis. Oberkommando des Heeres (Chief command of the army), Berlin. 1938.

125 Philip Johnson. Lincoln Center Plaza, New York. Draughtsman: Helmut Jacoby. 1958. Coloured pencils, waterproof.

126 Johnson/Burgee. The New Play House Theater, Cleveland, Ohio. Draughtsman: Bon-Hui-Uy. 1981. Pencil. $16 \times 30''$.

127 Venturi, Rauch and Scott Brown. Marlborough Blenheim Hotel and Casino, Atlantic City, New Jersey. Draughtsman: Stanford Hughes. 1977. Pencil.

128 Stanley Tigerman and Associates. "A kosher kitchen for a suburban Jewish American Princess" in Wilmette, Illinois. Draughtsman: Robert Caddigan. 1977. Ink and screen films.

129 Moore, Grover, Harper. Kingsmill on the James, Williamsburg, Virginia. Draughtsman: William Hersey. 1974. Ink.

130 Moore, Grover, Harper. St. Joseph's Fountain, Piazza d'Italia, New Orleans. Draughtsman: William Hersey and John Kyrk. 1979. Ink and pencil. $24 \times 36''$.

131 Robert Stern. Residence in East Hampton, New York. 1980.

132 Michael Graves. Kalko House, Green Brook, New Jersey. 1978. Pencil and coloured pencils, waterproof.

133 Michael Graves. Plocek House, Warren, New Jersey. 1979. Ink and coloured pencils. $8 \times 18''$.

134 Michael Graves. The Portland Building, Portland, Oregon. 1980. Ink and coloured pencils. $8 \times 8\frac{1}{2}''$.

135 Hans Hollein. Primary school in the Köhlergasse, Vienna. 1980. Fibre pen and sepia ink.

136 Friedrich St. Florian. Summer residence for Livia Campanella, Seccheto, Italy. Between 1973 and 1976. Ink and coloured pencils.

137 Mario Ridolfi. Lina House, Marmore, near Terni. 1966. Ink. $39\frac{3}{8} \times 27\frac{1}{2}''$.

138 Paolo Portoghesi. Roma/Amor. Draughtsman: Giampaolo Ercolani. 1978. Ink. $27\frac{1}{2} \times 27\frac{1}{2}''$. University of Parma.

139 James Stirling, Michael Wilford and Associates. School of Architecture, Rice University, Houston. Draughtsman: Paul Keogh. 1980. Pencil and wax crayons. $18 \times 18''$.

140 Taller de Arquitectura/Ricardo Bofill. Theatre in Marne-la-Vallée. Draughtsman: Patrick Dillon. 1980. Ink. $17\frac{3}{4} \times 23\frac{5}{8}''$.

141 Louis Kahn. Alfred Newton Richards Medical Research Building, University of Pennsylvania, Philadelphia. 1960.

142 Louis Kahn. Salk Institute for Biological Studies, La Jolla, California. Built in 1959–65.

143 Louis Kahn. Yale Center for British Art, New Haven, Connecticut. 1971. Graphite. $23\frac{7}{8} \times 31''$. The Louis I. Kahn Collection, University of Pennsylvania, Philadelphia.

144 James Stirling. Research and development centre of Siemens AG, München. Draughtsman: Leon Krier. 1969. Ink. $15 \times 19''$.

145 James Stirling. Town centre of Derby. Draughtsman: Leon Krier. 1970. Ink. $14 \times 7''$.

146 Arata Isozaki. Gunma Prefectural Museum of Fine Arts, Takasaki. 1976.

147 Arata Isozaki. Civic hall in Kamioka. 1978.

148 Josef Paul Kleihues. House for Markus Lüpertz. 1972. Pencil, ink and coloured pencils. $23\frac{1}{4} \times 28\frac{1}{8}''$.

149 Josef Paul Kleihues. House for Georg Baselitz. 1972. Pencil, ink and coloured pencils. $23\frac{1}{4} \times 28\frac{1}{8}''$.

150 Josef Paul Kleihues. Art Gallery Nordrhein-Westfalen, Düsseldorf. 1975. Pencil, ink and coloured pencils. $34\frac{1}{4} \times 46''$.

151 Oswald Mathias Ungers. Baden Library, Karlsruhe. Draughtsman: G. Wooding. 1979. Ink. $35\frac{1}{2} \times 41\frac{3}{8}''$.

152 Oswald Mathias Ungers. Exhibition hall in Frankfurt am Main. Draughtsman: G. Wooding. 1980. Ink. $32\frac{1}{4} \times 32\frac{1}{4}''$.

153 Rob Krier. Ideal plan for the Südliche Friedrichstadt, Berlin. Draughtsmen: Michael Bier and Rob Krier. 1977. Ink. $33\frac{1}{8} \times 46\frac{7}{8}''$.

154 Rob Krier. Schinkelplatz, Südliche Friedrichstadt, Berlin. 1980. Pencil and oil crayons.
$11^{7}/_{8} \times 8^{1}/_{4}''$.
155 Leon Krier. Project for Place Nôtre-
Dame, Amiens. 1975. Ink. $11^{7}/_{8} \times 8^{1}/_{4}''$.
156 Leon Krier. Project for Piazza San Pietro,
Rome. 1977. Ink.
157 Diana Agrest and Mario Gandelsonas.
Building 3, Buenos Aires. 1977.
158 Raimund Abraham. House without
Rooms. 1974/75. Pencil, coloured pencils and
photomontage. $14^{1}/_{8} \times 15^{3}/_{8}''$.
159 Mario Botta. Library of the Capuchin
convent in Lugano. Draughtsman: Martin
Boesch. 1979. Ink and screen films.
160 Bruno Reichlin and Fabio Reinhart.
Sartori House, Riveo, Switzerland. Draughtsman: Fabio Reinhart. 1975. Ink and airbrush.
161 Carlo Scarpa. Brion cemetery in San Vito
d'Altivole, Treviso. Built in 1969–75.
162 Gregotti Associati. University of Calabria,
Cosenza. 1973.
163 Giuseppe Grossi and Bruno Minardi.
Project for a piazza in Ancona. 1977/78. Ink.
$31^{1}/_{2} \times 43^{1}/_{4}''$.
164 Rodolfo Machado and Jorge Silvetti. The
Steps of Providence, Providence, Rhode
Island. Draughtsmen: Charles Crowley and
Steve Wanta. 1979. Ink. $22 \times 22''$.
165 Giorgio Grassi. San Pietro residential
unit, Abbiategrasso, near Milan. 1972. Ink and
fibre pen.
166 Giorgio Grassi. Restauration of the castle
in Abbiategrasso, near Milan. 1970. Ink.
167 Aldo Rossi. Building in the Gallaratese 2
housing complex, Milan. Draughtsman:
Massimo Fortis. 1968. Ink. Deutsches Archi-
tekturmuseum, Frankfurt am Main.
168 Aldo Rossi and Gianni Braghieri. Admin-
istration building in Trieste. Draughtsmen:
Gianni Braghieri and Max Bosshard. 1974.
Ink. $31^{1}/_{2} \times 39^{3}/_{8}''$. Deutsches Architektur-
museum, Frankfurt am Main.